Making Sense of Public Sector Investments

the 'five-case model' in decision making

Courtney A Smith

Economic Adviser
Department of Health

and

Joe Flanagan

Business Assurance Adviser
NHS Information Executive

Foreword by

Andy Carty

Partnerships UK (PUK)

RADCLIFFE MEDICAL PRESS

Radcliffe Medical Press Ltd
18 Marcham Road, Abingdon, Oxon OX14 1AA

British Library Cataloguing in Publication Data

A catalogue record for this book is available from the British Library.

ISBN 1 85775 432 8

Typeset by Aarontype Limited, Easton, Bristol
Printed and bound by TJ International Ltd, Padstow, Cornwall

Contents

Foreword

Everybody knows you need a business case to aid investment decisions. Some people know that using the 'five-case model' will improve that investment decision, but few people know the practicalities of how to construct a 'five-case model'.

This book is an invaluable tool for anybody needing to make investment decisions and for everyone who constructs a 'five-case model' this gives you a practical and easy to follow guide. But this is far more than a 'how to' guide – this book explains the ethos and reasoning, while giving easily understandable examples to help the readers comprehend why, as well as producing a rationale for investment.

This book is also timely, in that Government is going through a huge portfolio of change that is requiring, and in some cases demanding, departments to reconsider their whole raison d'etre and to enable cross-cutting, joined-up government. The only way we can be sure that these complicated interconnected and strategic issues are adequately dealt with is by progressing through a Strategic, Outline and then Full Business case. This book will instruct and guide you through that process!

Finally, during my time at Her Majesty's Treasury and in the private sector, I have seen too many expensive, and sometimes high profile, failures to be anything other than an unapologetic advocate for the 'five-case model'. In my experience there is nowhere else you will get the depth and breadth of understanding that is in this publication. Buy it, use it and prosper.

Andy Carty
Partnerships UK (PUK)
May 2001

About the authors

Courtney Smith is Economic Adviser in the Department of Health. He has held various posts in the Government Economic Service over the past 13 years, including Head of Portfolio Planning in the NHS Information Authority and Economic Adviser on PFI/PPP and capital investment issues in the NHS Executive. He has advised on PFI transactions with a capital value of some £2 billion within the health sector. His other books include *Making Sense of the Private Finance Initiative: developing public–private partnerships* (Radcliffe Medical Press, Oxford, 1999) and *Socialist Transformation in Peripheral Economies* (Avebury Press, Aldershot, 1995).

Joe Flanagan is currently Business Assurance Adviser to the NHS Information Authority. Prior to this appointment, he was Head of the Investment Proposal Service in the Central Computer and Telecommunications Agency (CCTA) in HM Treasury. Joe joined HM Treasury in 1972 and is the author of several best practice publications presently in use within the UK public sector. He has undertaken numerous assignments – helping to scope, plan, implement and review investment decisions – as lead consultant with a wide range of government departments and wider public sector organisations.

Acknowledgements

Our aim in writing this book is to provide a clear, authoritative and practical model to support capital investment decision making. We have successfully developed and tested the 'five-case model' over the past two years on a wide range of public sector projects. Use of the model for planning capital investments and structuring business cases has been adopted by the Office of Government Commerce (OGC), HM Treasury and is now mandatory in a number of government departments and agencies. It was mandated by the NHS Executive in September 2000 for NHS-generated information technology investments. It is now opportune to provide a definitive statement of the model to ensure that decision makers apply it properly.

We are grateful to all those who have participated in our seminars and workshops at which many of the ideas presented in the book were tested and refined. A number of individuals have also provided constructive feedback on earlier drafts or sections of the book.

Among those who deserve special mention are Nigel Bell, Baroness Noakes, Andy Burton, Andy Charlton, Neil Bruce Copp, Tony Dunstan, Brian Gardener, Colin Reeves, Clive Smee, Peter Coates, Andrew Lloyd-Kendall, John Guest, Francis Milner, Esther Collister, Hadyn Cook, John Farenden, Michael Flanagan, Keith Neil, Phil Saw, Jeremy Thorp, Sir David Walker Kt, Barry Williams and John Wright. For inspiration and moral support, we owe a special debt of gratitude to our relatives and friends, particularly the following individuals: Monica and Kenneth Baxter, Caroline Charlton, Lenora Clarke, Ayesha Dost, Stephen Dunn, Mark Figueroa, Barbara O'Leary, Naomi Smith, Jean Oni-Orisan, Ralph Lewars, Paul Sutton and Michael Witter. We also wish to thank the staff at Radcliffe Medical Press – Gillian Nineham, Jamie Etherington, Gregory Moxon, Natalie Butler and Angela Jones – for their forbearance and excellent technical support.

None of the individuals mentioned above nor their organisations should be held responsible for the views expressed in this book. As the lead author and editor, Courtney Smith takes responsibility for any errors of omission or commission which may be present.

Courtney A Smith
Joe Flanagan
April 2001

List of abbreviations

CBA   cost–benefit analysis
CITU   Central IT Unit
CSFs   critical success factors
DBFO   design, build, finance, operate
EHR   electronic health record
EPR   electronic patient record
EMU   European Monetary Union
FBC   full business case
G-CAT   government catalogue
HISS   hospital information support system
IM&T   information management and technology
IRR   internal rate of return
ITN   invitation to negotiate
ITT   invitation to tender
NPV   net present value
OBC   outline business case
OBS   output-based specification
OGC   Office of Government Commerce, HM Treasury
OJEC   Official Journal of the European Community
PFI   private finance initiative
PPP   public–private parternships
PRINCE   PRojects IN a Controlled Environment
PSC   public sector comparator
QALYs   quality-adjusted life years
RAM   risk allocation matrix
ROAMEF   rationale, objectives, appraisal, monitoring, evaluation, feedback
S-CAT   service catalogue
SMART   specific, measurable, achievable, relevant and timely
SOC   strategic outline case
SWOT   strengths, weaknesses, opportunities, threats
TUPE   Transfer of Undertakings (Protection of Employment)
           Regulations
VFM   value for money
WAN   wide area network

List of figures

To Barbara, Evelyn, Monica and Naomi Smith
from Courtney Smith

To Caroline, Joan and Joyce
from Joe Flanagan

Introduction

Background, scope and audience

This book presents a novel approach for planning and executing capital investments. The approach is loosely described as 'the five-case model'. The model addresses the core components of a robust investment appraisal – the 'strategic case' (business need and strategic fit), 'economic case' (generation of options and value-for-money assessment), 'commercial case' (the deal and supply-side capability), 'financial case' (affordability) and 'project management case' (achievability and deliverability). The comprehensive and holistic nature of the model ensures that all factors pertinent to the decision-making process are explicitly and systematically addressed.

The book reflects the experience we have gained over the years from advising on capital investment proposals and developing business plans. These cover a wide range of capital projects, particularly hospital buildings and information management and technology (IM&T).

Collectively, we have over 30 years of relevant experience in a number of public sector departments, including HM Treasury, Central Computer and Telecommunications Agency (CCTA), Cabinet Office, Department for Education and Employment, Department of Health and the NHS Information Authority. In addition, we have worked with a number of other public sector departments on developing technical guidance and imparting knowledge and skills on different facets of capital investment decision making.

We were instrumental in developing the idea of Strategic Outline Cases (SOCs), 'the five-case model' and the 'options framework', which underlie the 'economic case'. The book sets out to develop and demonstrate these ideas with applications to real case studies. Each chapter is guided by an explicit statement of the learning objectives and a summary of key messages. Frequent use is also made of checklists, answers to frequently asked questions and worked examples.

The model is generic and can be applied to a wide range of everyday decisions made by households, public and private sector organisations, and government. In this book, we will apply the model primarily to capital investment decisions. This includes replacement of existing assets, investment in new buildings, information management and technology, changes in managerial processes and general infrastructure.

However, the model can be applied in a straightforward manner to a wide range of other types of decisions, such as general business planning, mergers, acquisitions, expansion or diversification of product ranges and other 'business decisions'. It can also be applied to everyday decisions such as marriage, having children, housing decisions, labour market decisions, and the use of time and other resources.

Indeed, the model could justifiably be applied to the various situations discussed in Nobel laureate Gary Becker's pioneering work (1976) on *The Economic Approach to Human Behaviour*. Ultimately, it is a model for running a successful business, optimising the use of scarce resources and securing better outcomes from life. Businesses and individuals have to make decisions on an ongoing basis. All decisions involve the same fundamental process: comparison of alternatives and choosing the most advantageous course of action.

We share the firm conviction that proper deployment of this model will help to correct many of the current shortcomings of business planning and capital investment decision making within the public sector. Capital investment decisions should not be approached lightly. They rank among the most important decisions that public and private sector organisations have to make. Capital investment often requires a substantial outlay of the organisation's resources and commits it to a strategic path, which is difficult to change once the initial decision is made. At the same time, the returns from this type of investment are uncertain. Such investments are often dogged by a plethora of risks throughout the planning, development, construction, commissioning and operational stages.

It is well known that the performance of investment projects across the public sector is variable. Failure to deliver service requirements on time, within budget and to the required standard is common. This is borne out by the findings of various reviews undertaken by the National Audit Office and the number of failed projects that make newspaper headlines. Some of the more spectacular and widely debated examples include the Millennium Dome, the procurement of the National Insurance Recording System (NIRS2), the UK Passport Agency, the British Library and the Home Office's Case Recording and Management System.

The reasons for these failures are varied and complex. However, the evidence suggests that a common cause of suboptimal performance results from weaknesses in the way investment proposals are developed and implemented. Within the health sector, for example, concern about the problem and the inefficiencies in the business case and procurement process have attracted two reviews within the past four years – namely, 'The Root and Branch Review' and 'The NHS IM&T Procurement Review'. These reviews attribute the problem to the following factors:

- Incomplete understanding of the purpose of business cases and how this supports the organisation's corporate objectives.
- Lack of understanding of the external approval criteria and what information, analysis and detail are required to fulfil these requirements.
- Poor understanding of existing guidance, as well as deficiencies in some of the guidance.
- Lack of in-house capacity and resources (both skills and processes) for producing business cases and undertaking sound procurements.
- Failure to agree and communicate corporate objectives, strategic direction and business drivers.
- Failure to set the project within a wider strategic and business change context.
- Poor specification of project scope, objectives and desired service outcomes.
- A 'hit-and-miss' approach to the way options for satisfying the project objectives are identified and assessed.
- Poor information for populating the business case.
- Inadequate planning (failure to take into account all the milestones associated with the business case and procurement processes).
- Insufficient involvement and commitment from senior management and external stakeholders.
- Weak commercial focus and failure to adopt a strategic approach to the management of the market.
- Inadequate risk identification, assessment and management.

The last point is particularly significant. The experience of the Millennium Dome project may be used to illustrate this point. The project involved considerable financial risks, many of which were either not identified or not robustly assessed (*see* Case study below, with extracts from the National Audit Office's (NAO) Report on the project, November 2000, p. 20).

Case study: Risks faced by Millennium Dome project

Key risks identified	*What happened in practice*
Construction – the Dome might not be completed on time	The Dome opened on schedule (1 January 2000), but fitting out the Dome overran by three months. This meant there was limited opportunity for 'piloting' the Dome
Costs – Costs might exceed the May 1997 budget	The budget significantly overran

Demand – Visitor projections might be too high	The 12 million paying visitors projected did not materialise. Out-turn figure was approximately 50%
Marketing – Marketing might not sell the Dome to the public successfully, especially if it attracted negative publicity	The Dome was perceived by the public as a risky purchase, even though the majority of visitors actually enjoyed their experience
Ticket sales – The methods of selling tickets might not be successful and ticket prices may be too high	Visitor numbers were substantially short of what was anticipated
Sponsorship – Failure to secure anticipated levels of sponsorship, on account of delays in finalising contracts and unattractiveness of certain zones to sponsors	Sponsorship was lower than expected and, in some instances, failed to materialise
Sale proceeds – Buyers might not be found for the Dome, and an adequate selling price might not be achieved	A preferred bidder was announced in July 2000 but withdrew in September 2000. At the time of writing, a bidder is yet to be appointed

A number of these findings are further echoed in a recent Central IT Unit (CITU) report entitled *Successful IT: modernising government in action* (2000). The report offers 30 recommendations to improve the performance of public sector IM&T projects. The recommendations apply equally to projects outside the information technology sector.

The majority of these recommendations relate to the business case process, particularly the way projects are planned, appraised, implemented and managed. The report also stresses the importance of business-case skills, leadership and responsibility, risk management, benefit realisation, procurement and supplier relationships (see box, pp. 6–7).

With these concerns to the fore, our principal objective in writing this book is to improve understanding of all aspects of the decision-making process – from the inception of the proposal to project definition, analysis, selection, implementation and post-implementation review stages.

The primary audience includes senior managers, policy makers, politicians, practitioners and other personnel in government departments with responsibility for service delivery, business planning, producing and vetting business cases, and undertaking procurements. Management consultants, suppliers of goods and services to the public sector, and other private sector firms will also find the book of value. The book will also be of value to overseas interests.

The book will achieve its purpose if it leads to:

- demonstrable improvement in investment decisions and hence value for money
- speedier and more effective procurements
- more effective use of in-house and external advisers
- challenge, refinement or critique of the arguments presented
- proper deployment of the 'five-case model', the 'options framework', SOCs and economic appraisal techniques.

Framework of analysis and structure

The analysis is presented in ten chapters, arranged in three parts. Part one provides contextual and general guidance on the 'five-case model', the capital investment, business case and procurement processes. Part two unpacks the five-case model and provides detailed guidance on each of the five elements, while Part three is devoted to the production process, including the tools and techniques required to underpin the model.

More specifically, Chapter 1 provides an overview of the 'five-case model'. It also summarises the strengths of the model, the issues and the pitfalls to avoid in using the model. The potency of the model is illustrated in three contrasting case studies – joining the European Monetary Union, investing in a national electronic library and developing a new district general hospital. Other case studies are presented in ensuing chapters.

Chapter 2 provides an overview of the capital investment process and its fit with the 'five-case model' and the procurement process. It addresses the purpose and information requirements of SOCs, Outline Business Cases (OBCs) and Full Business Cases (FBCs). Emphasis is placed on SOCs on account of their novelty and the limited amount of available guidance.

Chapters 3 to 7 explain each element of the model. This is discussed in the following order – strategic case, economic case, commercial case, financial case and project management case. It is worth stressing from the outset that the model should not be viewed as a linear and mechanical construct. The various elements interact and are mutually reinforcing. The 'feedback loop' should be assessed and each of the five cases should be considered in the round.

Chapter 8 provides an exposition on investment appraisal methods, tools and techniques. It also summarises the strengths and weaknesses of the various approaches on offer, including pitfalls to avoid. Worked examples are provided to aid readers' understanding.

Chapter 9 clarifies the relationship between the business case and procurement process. It also provides an overview of the procurement process from OJEC (Official Journal of the European Community) advertisement to contract award, and provides a number of practical tips for managing the process to produce better and speedier procurements. Attention is also drawn to the merits of other non-traditional procurement arrangements, such as Government Catalogue (GCAT), Service Catalogue (SCAT) and e-procurement.

Chapter 10 reviews some of the 'process issues' that arise from producing and submitting the business case for approval within the public sector. It summarises approval thresholds, information sources for populating business cases, consultation with stakeholders, time-scales, the standard approval criteria (mapped on to the 'five-case model') and key 'gateway review' checkpoints. It concludes with a sample of comments volunteered by individuals and organisations who have used the five-case model for decision making.

The views expressed in this work are those of the authors and should not be attributed to the organisations to which they are affiliated. It does not represent official guidance or policy.

Extract of key recommendations from *Successful IT: modernising government in action*

- Business development skills must be included as a key feature in the extended Skills For the Information Framework which is being developed by CITU, the Office of Government Commerce (OGC) and the Centre for Management and Policy Studies.
- Business cases must reflect all of the business change to be delivered. Cross-cutting projects and programmes must have a single, integrated business case which is regularly updated and involve key stakeholders from the relevant organisations.
- Overall responsibility for delivering the business objectives and benefits of any programme or project must be vested in a single, responsible and visible Senior Responsible Officer (SRO).
- Key staff on major projects must undertake formal project management training which reflects their role in the project.
- Greater attention needs to be paid to risk analysis and risk management. To ensure effective risk management, procedures are needed to improve reporting and the upward referral of problems. This

should include peer reviews supported by clear guidelines and methods for problem reporting and upward referral.

- To mitigate the risks inherent in large and complex projects, departments and agencies should adopt a modular and/or incremental approach to project design, unless there are exceptional reasons to pursue a different approach.
- The outcomes from projects should be monitored and evaluated. The Office of Government Commerce should review the results of post-implementation reviews and disseminate the key results widely. A system of peer review will spread knowledge and ensure new projects draw on the available evidence.
- Departments and agencies should put in place suitable mechanisms to promote co-operation and open dialogue with suppliers. Before contracts are signed, suppliers must produce a realistic plan for how they will deliver services to meet the client's requirements.

Source: Central IT Unit (2000) *Successful IT: modernising government in action.* Cabinet Office, London.

PART ONE

Context and framework

CHAPTER ONE

Overview of the 'five-case model'

This chapter presents an overview of the 'five-case model'. It also summarises the strengths of the model, the issues and the pitfalls to avoid in its application. As a decision-making framework, the model is very powerful. Its potency is illustrated in three case studies – joining the European Monetary Union, investing in a national electronic library and developing a new hospital in Halifax. Other case studies relating to standard capital investment decisions are also presented in ensuing chapters.

The model

The 'five-case' model provides a systematic and comprehensive framework for decision making, particularly capital investment decisions. The framework ensures that the preferred option which results from the various analyses satisfies the following crucial tests:

- applicability to business needs and strategic direction
- optimum value for money
- attractiveness to the marketplace
- affordability to the organisation
- achievability in terms of time-scale, resources and other business parameters.

The model comprises five complementary segments:

- strategic case
- economic case
- commercial case
- financial case
- project management case.

These broadly mirror the main functional units present in modern organ-isations: planning and corporate affairs (strategic dimension), finance and purchasing (economic and financial dimensions), production and market-ing (commercial dimension), and organisational development and human resource (project management dimension).

Viewed from another perspective, the model mirrors the five sets of key strategic issues which all businesses need to address if they are to prosper (Table 1.1).

Table 1.1: Key strategic issues and the 'five-case model'

Key strategic issues	The 'five-case model'
Where are we now and where do we want to be?	Strategic case
What are the available options for getting us there? Which is the best route to adopt?	Economic case
Can we afford to get there within the given time-scale?	Financial case
Who is going to help us to get there?	Commercial case
How will we ensure we get there? Will we know when we have got there?	Project management case

The model is driven by users' needs. After all, organisations exist to meet the needs of their 'customers'. They need to produce the right products and services in the most cost effective way; with the right skills mix and other inputs; and deliver products and services to users to time, budget and quality. The five-case model is geared towards sound planning to meet this requirement. We will now explain each element in turn.

The strategic case

This forces the organisation's board of directors and other decision makers to subject their solutions to perceived or actual problems to an 'applica-bility test'. Will the solution meet the business needs? Is it consistent with the organisation's strategic direction and vision? Box 1.1 provides a more general list of the key issues which must be considered under the strategic case.

Box 1.1: Scope of strategic case

Strategic context
Organisational overview
Existing business strategies
The case for change – strategic needs
Existing arrangements
Business needs – current and future (defined in terms of outputs
    and outcomes)
Investment objectives
Potential scope and service requirements
Benefits criteria
Business risks
Constraints and dependencies

The economic case

Apart from death and taxes, the only certainty in life is scarcity of resources. Organisations therefore need to allocate resources efficiently, economically and effectively.

The economic case is designed to ensure that the preferred solution optimises value for money. This means that alternatives (hereafter termed options) must always be considered and evaluated against relevant criteria. The aim should be to identify the course of action that will maximise the ratio of benefits to costs. Options need to be robustly identified, assessed and eliminated.

One of the main weaknesses of investment appraisal practice within the public sector is failure to consider a wide range of options to meet the investment objectives and to assess the options objectively and systematically. To correct this shortcoming, we have developed 'the options framework' to tease out and ensure all relevant options are identified and systematically analysed.

The options framework is discussed in detail in Chapter 4. It generates options in terms of five parameters:

- scope (degree of business change required)
- service solution (solutions set including technical requirements)
- implementation (timing, phasing and degree of 'modularity')
- service delivery (organisational vehicle for delivering the requirement: single organisation, collaborative approaches, etc.)

- sources of funds (exchequer, private finance, sponsorship, mixed funding, etc.).

The scope of the economic case is outlined in Box 1.2.

Box 1.2: Scope of economic case

Critical success factors

Long-listed options (drawing an options framework)
Potential scopes
Potential service solution
Potential methods of service delivery
Potential implementation scenarios
Potential funding methods
Preferred way forward

Short-listed options (four is the recommended number)
Baseline – status quo; do nothing; do minimum
The public sector comparator
Other short-listed options

Economic appraisals
Net present value results
Benefits appraisal
Risks assessment
Sensitivity analysis

The preferred option and reasons for recommendation

The commercial case

Most decisions will also have commercial and contractual implications. Modern-day organisations are not self-sufficient. They rely on markets to supply their 'factors of production' – property, information technology, other assets, labour, raw materials, finance and the like. Organisations, therefore, need to consider the 'supply-side' dimension of their proposals. It must pass an 'attractiveness test'. Will their proposals be 'attractive' to suppliers? Will it result in a win–win commercial deal? Will it pass the 'bankability test' (in the case of third-party-financed projects)? Are the risks allocated optimally between the various parties? Is the chosen supplier(s) able to successfully deliver the requirements of the contract? Does the deal make sense?

Box 1.3: Scope of the commercial case

Scope and services
Charging mechanisms
Risk transfer
Key contractual arrangements
Personnel (TUPE) implications
Accountancy treatment
Other relevant information about the deal

The financial case

This is designed to ensure any proposed solutions pass the 'affordability test'. Can the organisation afford the cost implications of the solutions on offer when assessed in terms of its available 'income' and ongoing 'expenditure'? Is the deal affordable in both the short-run and long-run? The financial case should not be confused with the 'economic case'. As noted before, the economic case is concerned with options appraisal and value for money. The costs, benefits and risks analysed as part of the economic case go beyond the organisational level. Economists generally agree that they should be viewed at the societal level to ensure that both private and social costs and benefits are assessed. Apart from the 'spatial' dimension, it is also worth noting that the financial case includes both resource and non-resource costs. A good example of the latter is indirect taxation and other 'transfer payments'.

Box 1.4: Scope of the financial case

Public capital requirements
Net effect on prices
Impact on balance sheet
Impact on income & expenditure account
Overall affordability
Letter of support from 'funders'

The project management case

This boils down to 'achievability' and 'deliverability'. It is designed to address issues such as:

- Will the proposed solution meet the business needs within the desired time-scale, available resources and other business parameters?
- Are sound arrangements in place to identify and manage risks?
- Has adequate thought been given to benefit realisation?
- Are there arrangements for ongoing monitoring, post-implementation review, contract management and general project management?
- Have all critical success factors been identified?
- Is there a strategy for managing risks throughout the life of the project?

Box 1.5: Scope of the project management case

The procurement plan
The project methodology and structure
The project plan
Use of advisors
Contract management
Benefits realisation
Risk management
Post-project evaluation

Interpreting the model

Models are theoretical constructs that capture the essence of the phenomenon under investigation. It is a way of organising our thinking and approach to solving a problem. Of necessity, a model has to abstract from the complexities of reality, just as a map has to omit some of the details of the landscape.

This does not mean it distorts reality. If it distorts reality, its explanatory and predictive power will be weak. This would render the model invalid. The skill is to strike the right balance between simplicity and complexity.

As with all models, the 'five-case model' needs to be used with care. Users should resist the temptation to interpret the model in a linear and mechanical manner. **The five elements of the model are closely inter-related**. For example, the business need articulated as part of the strategic case should take account of the financial case, particularly the affordability envelope within which the service solution needs to be met. Value for money is the product not just of the economic case but all five cases. For example, if the need is wrongly specified, the right options will not be identified and assessed. Even if the right option is selected, it needs to be procured and implemented cost-effectively. This has implications for the development of the procurement strategy, the management of the tendering process, the evaluation of bids and the negotiation of contracts.

A change in any of the five cases will impact on the remaining four. Imagine we have established a suitably comprised multidisciplinary team to complete the five cases. However, shortly after the work has been completed, a new government policy has been announced which has the effect of increasing demand for the organisation's services by over 30%. This may be interpreted as a change in the strategic context. Clearly, the organisation would need to revisit the economic case to ensure the preferred option remains valid. The commercial case, financial case and project management case would similarly need to be reviewed to restore 'equilibrium'.

Schematically, the model may be presented as shown in Figure 1.1 below. Note the direction of the relationships.

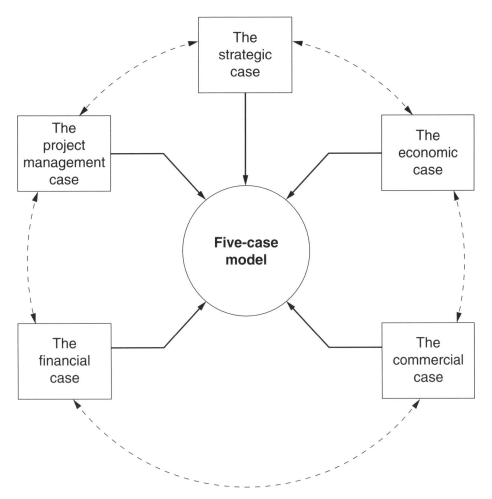

Figure 1.1: Schematic representation of the 'five-case model'.

Applications of the model

The model is robust and comprehensive. To date, the authors have applied it to the planning of a number of IM&T investments in the NHS Information Authority, Northern Ireland Prison Service, Health and Safety Executive, Ministry of Defence, Inland Revenue, Scottish Office and Welsh Office, among others. The model has now been adopted by the NHS Executive and Office of Government Commerce, HM Treasury for wider use across the public sector.

We will illustrate briefly the analytical power of the model with the use of three case studies, one of which is unconventional. As noted before, the model could justifiably be applied to the various situations discussed in Gary Becker's pioneering work (1976) on *The Economic Approach to Human Behaviour*.

Writing about the power of the 'economic framework', Becker argues:

> I applied the economic approach to fertility, education, the uses of time, crime, marriage, social interactions, and other 'sociological', 'legal', and 'political' problems. Only after long reflection on this work and the rapidly growing body of related work by others did I conclude that the economic approach was applicable to all human behaviour (p. 8).

Although controversial, the same could be said about the generality of the 'five-case model'. All decisions involve the same fundamental process: comparison of alternatives and choosing the most advantageous course of action, i.e. the 'preferred option'. There are costs and 'consequences' (i.e. benefits and dis-benefits) arising from the various options on offer. These need to be evaluated. We suggest that an appraisal in the spirit of cost-benefit analysis will lead to better decision making. We will now illustrate how the 'five-case model' can be applied to common, everyday decisions.

Case study 1: Should Britain relinquish its national currency and join the European Monetary Union?

Before turning to capital investment decisions, let us for instance consider the controversial issue of whether Britain should relinquish its national currency and join the European Monetary Union (EMU). The model suggests the decision makers should analyse this issue *in the round* from five perspectives:

Strategic case

- What are the objectives of the EMU project?
- How important are these objectives to Britain?
- Do they complement Britain's economic and wider political strategy?
- Is there a compelling and urgent need for Britain to join?
- Is it in Britain's short-term and long-term interest to join?
- What would be lost from not joining?
- What would be gained from joining?
- Would the nation's *net welfare* increase as a result of joining?
- Have the British population and other relevant 'stakeholders' been consulted about whether or not to join the EMU? Are there provisions for a referendum and/or other consultative arrangements?
- What are the prevailing constraints and dependencies?

Economic case

- What are the available options for meeting the EMU objectives?
- Has consideration been given to a wide range of options?
- Does this include, for example, 'implementation and timing' options (i.e. incremental versus big bang), scoping options (a narrow EU co-operating on a limited range of policies such as free trade versus a wide EU encompassing the whole of Europe co-operating on a wide range of economic, social and political policies?)
- Is there a do nothing (status quo) and do minimum option (e.g. preparatory work to join at a later stage)?
- What are the economic costs and benefits associated with the different options identified?
- What are the non-economic costs and benefits?
- What are the risks?
- How do the costs, benefits and risks change over time?
- Are there differences between short- and long-run outcomes?
- Is there any empirical evidence to support the costs, benefits and risks identified?
- How relevant is evidence from other monetary unions?
- Has allowance been made for any important differences in the labour market, financial markets, housing, legal, fiscal and other institutions prevailing between Britain and the rest of the EU?
- What difference does the openness of the economy make to the costs, benefits and risks?
- What is the preferred option and recommendations from this analysis?
- On what basis is the preferred option chosen?

Commercial case

- Have the key commercial issues been identified and assessed?
- Are these reflected in a clear 'contract' and institutional framework? (The Maastricht Treaty may be viewed as an attempt to address the 'commercial case'. This sets out the basic parameters of the EMU 'deal'.)
- Does the 'deal' take into account the differing and changing needs of the member states?
- Are there suitable sanctions and change control mechanisms in place?

Financial case

- Can Britain afford the short-run and long-run costs of the project?
- Can it afford not to join the project?
- What is the best way to finance the project?
- What are the risks of default on a debt once in the EMU?

Project management case

- Is the project supported by effective institutional, accountability and project management arrangements?
- Are there suitable regulatory controls in place?
- Are there suitable mechanisms for resolving policy conflicts and asymmetric shocks?
- What are the issues arising from the transition to a single currency?
- What are the key risks to be managed?
- How best might these be managed?
- Is there a clear monetary policy strategy for realising the desired outcome for inflation, economic growth and other economic targets?
- What are the roles and responsibilities of national government and the different regulation bodies?
- Can the benefits be realised given differences in labour market and other institutions?
- Are there suitable plans in place to monitor and evaluate the effects of the decision to join or not to join?

Until these issues are confronted head-on, the controversy over joining the EMU will continue to abound.

Case study 2: Should Calderdale Healthcare NHS Trust develop a new hospital in Halifax?

This case study uses extracts from the Calderdale Healthcare NHS Trust's business case to illustrate the basic principles of the 'five-case model'. It is not intended to be comprehensive. The new £77m capital development was the fifth major hospital to be procured under the PFI (*see* Smith, 1999)

Strategic case

What is wrong with the status quo?

Acute, elderly and mental health services are split between three sites. Several clinical adjacencies are not achieved, thus resulting in the following deficiencies:

- outpatient services and operating theatres are fragmented across and within sites;
- the Accident and Emergency department is on a separate site from the Critical Care Unit, acute medical, acute elderly, paediatric medicine, obstetric, gynaecology and acute mental health beds
- paediatric medicine and surgery are on separate sites
- elderly and mental health beds are on a site with minimal diagnostic and therapeutic services and with poor access for the majority of local people
- concentration of capital resources on acute services with limited investment in community settings even though inpatient length of stay is on a downward trend.

> As well as impacting adversely on the clinical quality of care, split site working has a significant impact on the costs of providing care. It also creates staffing difficulties, e.g. achieving cover for junior doctors. It makes the efficient use of beds and other facilities difficult, raising costs unnecessarily.
>
> Moreover, the capital stock is in urgent need of modernisation. Most of the buildings were built over 100 years ago by the Halifax Poor Union and Public Subscription. This results in major inefficiencies in space utilisation, major health and safety shortfalls, inefficient energy use and high maintenance costs. It is estimated that £52.1m (1996 price base) is needed to bring the estate to an acceptable physical, statutory and energy standard, marginally improving the space utilisation, whilst leaving the problems of fragmentation intact.

The Trust recognised that it could not meet its strategic objectives and wider government priorities without a major reconfiguration of its services and estate. The Trust specified a wide range of objectives which include:

- to achieve the significant development of care in community-based settings
- to provide a local secondary care centre of excellence to deliver complex specialist medical services in support of primary care and community-based practitioners
- to ensure that hospital admission only takes place where it is necessary and that GPs are provided with accessible support services
- to work with the Local Authority to jointly plan and provide 'Care in the Community' services
- to structure provision towards improving health outcomes in line with local priorities and the challenges of *Our Healthier Nation*
- to manage resources to achieve levels of efficiency and effectiveness compatible with current best practice and national targets.

Economic case

What are the available options for meeting the investment objectives?

Taking into account the needs of the local population, national and local priorities, its longer-term objectives and the potential of the existing estate, the Trust generated a wide range of options. These include:

Option 1: Do nothing
Option 2: Do minimum
Option 3: Surgical services at Royal Halifax Infirmary and medical and non-acute services at Halifax General Hospital
Option 4: All hospital services at Halifax General Hospital
Option 5: All hospital services at Royal Halifax Infirmary
Option 6: All hospital services on a greenfield site
Option 7: Acute services at Halifax General Hospital and non-acute services at Royal Halifax Infirmary
Option 8: Surgical services at Halifax General Hospital and medical and non-medical services at Royal Halifax Infirmary
Option 9: Hospital services at Halifax General Hospital with restricted trauma facilities
Option 10: Three community Resource Centres but no hospital in Calderdale.

Following a high-level appraisal, the following four options were short-listed for a more rigorous assessment:

Option 1:   Do Nothing (retained for baseline comparison)
Option 2:   Do Minimum
Option 4:   All hospital services at Halifax General Infirmary (the best single site option)
Option 7:   Acute services at Halifax General Infirmary and non-acute services at Royal Halifax Infirmary (the best two site option).

At the OBC stage, Option 4 emerged as the preferred option, based on the results of the discounted cash flow analysis, assessment of non-financial benefits, risks and comprehensive sensitivity analysis.

This option was developed as the Trust's public sector comparator. It was tested during the procurement stage to determine the best method of funding – public finance *versus* private finance under the aegis of the PFI. The PFI option produced a lower net present cost by a significant margin and was, consequently, chosen as the best value for money option.

Under the PFI option, the Trust transferred a significant amount of risk to the Consortium. Examples of the risks transferred include:

- overruns on construction costs
- costs of latent defects
- escalating maintenance and repair costs
- income generation schemes failing to net income targets
- losses arising from unavailability of any aspect of facilities and support services.

Commercial case

What are the main features of the proposed deal?

Supported by its legal, financial and technical advisers, the Trust advertised the project in the *Official Journal of the European Community* and sought competitive bids in line with the government's Private Finance Initiative. Catalyst, a non-recourse Special Purpose Company, was selected as preferred partner.

The deal agreed with Catalyst formed the basis of the contract. The contract was divided into two phases: the design and construction stage (phase 1) and the concession period during which Catalyst will make the hospital and its services available to the Trust (phase 2). The second phase extends to 60 years, with an option for the Trust to terminate the concession after 30, 40 or 50 years.

Other issues addressed in the contract include: payment mechanism, indexation, benchmarking and market testing, legislative changes, delay events, compensation events, relief events, TUPE/human resources issues, expiry or earlier termination of the contract and corrupt gifts.

Financial case

Is the preferred option affordable?

An affordability analysis was conducted on each of the short-listed options to demonstrate the impact of the investment on the Trust's income and expenditure position. This analysis took account of the full cost of each option, including non-recoverable VAT and capital charges. Apart from a minor affordability gap in year 1, the analysis reveals that the PFI option was affordable and delivered a net reduction (−) on current baseline costs.

As shown in Table 1.2, this option generated the largest quantum of savings for reinvestment in local healthcare services, particularly development of community services. The Trust's main purchaser, Calderdale and Kirklees Health Authority, fully supported the PFI option.

Table 1.2: Summary results from affordability analysis

Net impact on prices	Do minimum (£000)	Public sector comparator (£000)	PFI option (£000)
Year 1	639	1143	39
Year 10	639	1143	−809
Year 20	639	1143	−1052

Project management case

Have suitable arrangements been put in place to manage the various stages of the project?

From the outset, the Trust established a suitably comprised Project Board to oversee the project, based on PRINCE project management methodology. Members of the Board contributed to the development of the contract management strategy, benefit realisation plan, risk management strategy, monitoring and evaluation plans, and the communication strategy. The project management arrangements, including supporting plans and timetables, were summarised in the Trust's business case.

Case Study 3: Should the NHS Information Authority develop a digital library (National electronic Library for Health, NeLH)?

Strategic case

- What is the strategic and policy fit for the NeLH (*see* Box 1.6)?
- What are the existing arrangements for library services – both traditional and digital?
- What are the limitations of these arrangements?
- What are the investment objectives?
- What are the key constraints and dependencies?
- What are the desired outcomes from investment in a NeLH?
- What is the appropriate scope for the NeLH (if these outcomes are to be delivered)?

Box 1.6: Strategic fit for NeLH

- NeLH is a key strand of *Information for Health* and the Government's Modernisation Programme.
- It will revolutionise the way information is used and support delivery of patient care.
- It supports the National Plan.
- It supports the Government's strategic framework for public service in the information age: e-citizens, e-business, e-government.
- It complements other information-related initiatives in the NHS (e.g. National Service Frameworks).

Economic case

- What are the options for meeting the investment objectives (both long-list and short-list)?
- Has consideration been given to scoping, technical, implementation, service delivery and funding options?
- What are the critical success factors for evaluating the options?
- What are the resulting short-listed options?
- What are the relative advantages and disadvantages of the short-listed options?

- What are the costs, benefits and risks associated with the short-listed options?
- Have the results of the economic appraisal been tested via suitable sensitivity analysis?
- What is the preferred option?
- What are the reasons for choosing this option as the preferred way forward?

Commercial case

- How will the NeLH be procured?
- Will there be different contracts for content, software, hardware and services such as helpdesk and training?
- What procurement route will be adopted (e.g. PFI)?
- What are the key risks and will they be apportioned between the NHS Information Authority and the private sector?
- What is the proposed charging mechanism?
- What is the desired duration of the contract(s)?
- What are the desired terms and conditions for the contract?

Financial case

- What is the value of the contract(s) for the NeLH?
- How does this compare with the budget allocated for the NeLH?
- Is the contract for the NeLH affordable year on year?
- How will affordability pressures be met?
- Is the financial case supported by a rigorous affordability analysis (including sensitivity tests)?

Project management case

- What are the critical success factors for the NeLH (*see* Box 1.7)?
- How will these activities be managed?
- What management structures will be put in place to manage the NeLH?
- What are the respective roles and responsibilities of the various parties?
- How will benefits be managed?
- What are the main characteristics of the benefit realisation plan?
- What are the main features of the training plan?

> **Box 1.7:** Key activities for successful delivery of the NeLH
>
> - Procurement of servers, hardware, software and connectivity
> - Delivery of Access Management System for all users
> - Website design
> - Content licensing
> - Service delivery (including management of a number of contracts)
> - Evaluation
> - Virtual branch libraries and benefit realisation
> - Training
> - Search engine
> - Public access (including liaison with NHS Direct Online)
> - Office and administration
> - Communication
> - Risks

- What arrangements will be made for monitoring and evaluating the NeLH?
- What are the main features of the communication strategy for the NeLH?
- How will lessons from evaluation and the project as a whole be disseminated?

The business case for the pilot NeLH was based on the five-case model. It may be viewed online at www.nelh.nhs.uk.

Mapping the model on to the approval criteria

Another dimension on the power of the model is how well it fits with the standard approval and 'gateway review' criteria adopted by departments and public watchdog bodies such as HM Treasury, the NAO and the OGC.

This is discussed in greater detail in Chapter 10. For illustrative purposes, however, all proposals would normally be expected to satisfy the following core, high-level requirements (*see* Table 1.3).

Skills implications

The model has implications for assembling project teams to ensure the project is soundly developed and the decision-making process is robust at each stage in the process. By definition, the model suggests the adoption of

Table 1.3: Core high-level approval requirements

Strategic Issues

- Is there a compelling service need for the investment?
- Are the project objectives and desired benefits clearly specified?
- Are dependencies clearly identified?
- Is the project properly scoped?
- Are all stakeholders appropriately consulted?

Value-for-money issues

- Are all available options for meeting the investment objectives and service need considered?
- Are the options appraised properly and fairly (proper identification and assessment of costs, benefits and risks)?
- Is the best value for money option chosen?
- Will this option meet government and departmental objectives?
- Have all underlying options been verified and tested?

Commercial issues

- Is the project supported by a sound procurement strategy?
- Has the procuring organisation followed the appropriate procurement process?
- Have all bids been treated fairly and in line with the relevant procurement guidelines?
- Has the best value for money solution been chosen?
- Is the contract developed in line with best practice?

Affordability issues

- Is the deal affordable in the short- and long-term?
- Is it supported by the Board and the relevant 'commissioners'?
- Have suitable sensitivity analyses been performed?
- Are resources in place to close any expected or unexpected affordability gap?

Project management issues

- Are there adequate arrangements in place to manage the project?
- Has sufficient attention been paid to risk management, benefit realisation, contract management, post-implementation review and other critical success factors?
- Is there evidence of senior management involvement and commitment?
- Is the project 'owned' by a SRO?

a suitably comprised **multidisciplinary team**. The main skills requirements are discussed in Chapter 10.

In brief, skills and knowledge will be needed in each functional area to reflect the 'five-case model'. In broad terms, the following skills are required:

- Strategic case – strategic planning, business planning, leadership, performance management, facilitation, people management and technical skills to reflect the type of project (e.g. estate, survey and engineering skills in the case of building schemes).
- Economic case – generation of options, investment appraisal, risk analysis, general economics and operational research skills.
- Commercial case – commercial, negotiating, legal and finance skills.
- Financial case – corporate finance and accountancy skills.
- Project management case – leadership and project management skills.

Concluding remarks

The key points from this chapter may be summarised as follows.

- Capital investment decisions or, for that matter, any decision should be analysed in the round.
- The 'five-case model' provides a systematic and proven approach for ensuring investment decisions are properly and comprehensively analysed.
- The model suggests such decisions should best be made by a multidisciplinary team to ensure all relevant issues – strategic, economic, commercial, financial and project management – are considered.
- Before making the investment decision, you must ensure the investment fits the organisation's strategic direction, the best value for money option has been chosen, the investment is commercially attractive to suppliers, it is affordable and will be soundly managed.
- Considerable care must be taken in applying the model. It should not be used as a linear, mechanical and rigid drill.

CHAPTER TWO

The 'five-case model' and the capital investment process

This chapter provides an overview of the capital investment process and its fit with the 'five-case model'. It addresses the purpose and information requirements of Strategic Outline Cases, Outline Business Cases and Full Business Cases. Emphasis is placed on Strategic Outline Cases on account of their novelty and the limited amount of documented guidance on this stage in the business case process.

Overview of the capital investment and business case process

The ultimate aim of capital investment is to increase returns to 'stakeholders' over and above what could have been gained in the next best alternative. In the private sector, the main stakeholders are shareholders. In the public sector, the intended beneficiaries are the public.

To maximise returns to stakeholders, decisions made at each stage in the investment process need to be robust. The decision-making process also needs to be supported by the right type of information and supporting analysis. Just as there are different stages in the capital investment process, there are also distinct stages in the business case process. This section summarises the capital investment process. The ensuing section discusses the information and business case requirement associated with the key stages of the investment process. It is worth stressing from the outset that each subsequent stage in the capital investment process requires greater commitment from senior managers. As we progress down the 'commitment chain', the information requirement will generally increase.

The capital investment process typically involves six distinct, but complementary, stages. The main stages are:

- **Stage 1: Generation of proposals.** This is the 'triggering stage'. Each opportunity for product or service development must first be identified. It is important for investment ideas to be consistent with the organisation's strategic direction.

- **Stage 2: Initial screening of ideas.** Once the idea is generated, it needs to be developed sufficiently so that its merits can be assessed.

- **Stage 3: Project definition and analysis.** If the idea passes the 'screening test' and receives initial 'go-ahead', further definition is required to facilitate a more rigorous assessment of its viability.

- **Stage 4: Selection.** Based on pre-determined criteria, information submitted and supporting analysis, the organisation has to decide what priority and resources, if any, to assign to the idea.

- **Stage 5: Implementation.** Proposals which satisfy the various criteria and assessments must now be resourced and implemented. Implementation may take a range of forms, varying from proto-
- types to full-scale implementation.

- **Stage 6: Monitoring and evaluation.** Resources also need to be set aside to monitor and evaluate the economy, efficiency and effectiveness of the original idea. Was it a good idea in the first instance? Do the actual outcomes mirror the projected outcomes?

The evolution of the business case

As noted earlier, each stage of the capital investment process needs to be supported with appropriate information, analysis and documentation. Three levels of analysis or types of business cases are pertinent to the decision-making process. These are the SOC, OBC and FBC.

We will concentrate on the SOC, as the other two stages are well established. The general purpose of OBCs and FBCs and the criteria for judging their quality are set out in the Department of Health's *Capital Investment Manual* (1994) and HM Treasury's 'Green Book' – *Appraisal and Evaluation in Central Government* (1997). The seminal work on SOCs has been conducted by Smith (2000) in a publication entitled *Maximising Value for Money: examining the role of Strategic Outline Cases.*

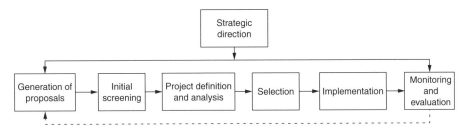

Figure 2.1: The capital investment process.

It is worth stressing at the outset that the business case process should be viewed as a single process which evolves to support decision making throughout the whole capital investment cycle. This is illustrated in Figure 2.1. At the screening stage, SOCs will typically be required to determine whether preliminary proposals are in keeping with the organisation's overall business strategy. Once the initial go-ahead has been given to define the proposal in greater detail, an OBC may be required to decide on whether the project still warrants commitment and resources from senior managers within and outside the organisation. Before the contract award and implementation stage, a FBC will normally be required to confirm that the tendering process has been soundly managed and that the proposal is still able to meet the requirements for value for money, affordability and achievability.

Beyond this stage, there will be a need for other 'gateway reviews' and analyses to facilitate the decision-making process. These include:

● The 'readiness' of the organisation to award and implement the contract.
● The monitoring, reviewing and evaluation phase.

The results from the post-implementation review should feed back into the process to identify further investment opportunities and to improve their design, development, implementation and management.

It should be clear from the preceding discussion that the business case is a 'live', 'evolutionary' management tool. The term 'evolutionary' is used advisedly. The progression from strategy to SOC, to OBC to FBC is analogous to the stages in 'human development'. The SOC broadly corresponds with the stages up to birth of the 'newborn child'. The OBC reflects the 'childhood phase' and the FBC may be likened to the 'adulthood phase'. Despite growth and development, all of this represents a single process. This analogy also throws into sharp relief the different 'levels of detail' which characterise SOCs, OBCs and FBCs. As a proposal develops momentum and progresses down the 'commitment chain', the decision-making process requires more detailed and reliable information. FBCs are, therefore, characterised by rigorous analyses. OBCs are based on 'indicative' analyses and SOCs by 'very high-level order of magnitude' analyses.

This view of business cases as a 'live, evolutionary management tool' is not shared by all organisations. Partly on account of weaknesses in the way business cases are centrally regulated, there is a tendency for some project initiators in the public sector to view the business case process as a series of hoops which organisations have to go through in order to secure approval for major expenditures. There is also evidence of organisations 'unbundling' major procurements and making suboptimal decisions in order to bypass the approval regime.

Box 2.1 indicates some of the purposes which the business-case process ought to serve.

Box 2.1: A positive view of business cases

A business case, if approached positively, can serve a number of useful purposes. It:

- forces decision makers to consider all the available options, thus providing an explicit and systematic basis for decision making
- promotes accountability for the use of resources
- provides an audit trail to facilitate assessment of whether public resources have been used efficiently and effectively
- provides a vehicle for involving stakeholders in the planning of the investment and securing commitment at all levels
- clarifies the service need and informs the procurement process
- inspires confidence in suppliers in the organisation's ability to deliver their side of the 'partnership'. A business case provides evidence that affordability and other important aspects of the project have been clearly thought through
- provides a basis for post-implementation review
- serves as a live management tool to assess whether the project is operating within the original parameters and is producing the desired impact.

Strategic outline case

The SOC is the first stage in the business-case process. SOCs represent a new stage in the planning cycle. They were first introduced in the NHS

Executive in the past three years to facilitate the planning and prioritisation of major capital schemes. The main rationale for their introduction was to improve the planning of such schemes, ensure they were driven by service needs (hence the focus on strategic issues), and to avoid wasting scarce resources developing detailed business cases which stood little chance of attracting funding and commitment from key stakeholders.

So far they have not been applied extensively to IM&T projects. In the wake of a growing number of failed IM&T projects throughout the public sector and the findings of the NAO's recent review of the design and implementation of the Department of Health's 1992 and 1998 IM&T strategies, consideration is now being given to extending SOCs to IM&T projects. This has been further reinforced by a number of recommendations in the recent NHS Procurement Review.

Regardless of the nature of the project, the main purpose of a SOC is to establish the business need for the proposed intervention and any resulting investment. It should explain clearly the service drivers for the project and how it satisfies ministerial and other policy priorities.

SOCs are particularly useful in situations where:

- there are a large number of disparate stakeholders involved in a project or change management initiative
- the project is novel, risky and complex
- the parameters of the project are ill-defined (particularly the objectives and scope).

There are many circumstances in which these conditions hold, particularly in the area of information technology and the advent of cross-cutting procurements in support of joined-up government and the national e-commerce strategy (UK On-line). In such circumstances, the SOC provides an opportunity for the stakeholders to quickly survey the issues which would normally be addressed in detail in an OBC. As a result of this overview of the key issues, it is possible to tighten the scope and objectives of the project, identify options for satisfying the objectives and (based on a high-level assessment, e.g. a qualitative assessment of the strengths and weaknesses of each option) decide how best to proceed.

Outline business case

The OBC builds on the SOC. Its primary purposes are to:

- Identify and validate the preferred option for meeting the project objectives.

- Demonstrate that this option is likely to be attractive to suppliers and at the same time pass the value-for-money (VFM), affordability and achievability tests.
- Inform the procurement process.
- Secure commitment and funding from the relevant stakeholders and decision makers to implement the project.

The typical issues addressed in the OBC may be summarised as follows:

- What is wrong with the status quo? What are the drivers for the investment? What is it seeking to achieve?
- Given there is a compelling case for change, what are the available options for meeting the business need?
- How do the costs, benefits and risks of the short-listed options compare? Which is the best value for money option?
- Is the preferred option affordable?
- Are the benefits from the investment understood? Have they been identified and supported by an initial benefit realisation plan?
- Is it likely to be attractive to suppliers?
- How will the preferred option be procured and managed? What is the procurement strategy and plan? Is the timetable realistic?
- Have all critical success factors for completing the project been identified?
- Is there a strategy in place to manage risks? Have the key risks been identified?

Guidance on how to address these issues is provided in the ensuing chapters. The level of detail is a matter for judgement. Appendix 2 summarises the issues which should be addressed in an OBC. The contents and degree of detail are compared and contrasted with the requirements for a SOC and a FBC.

Full business case

The FBC updates the issues addressed in the OBC. In addition, it documents the results of the procurement process. It seeks to unambiguously identify the preferred option for meeting the requirements of the project.
  The FBC must convincingly demonstrate that:

- The business need for the investment remains valid.
- The investment still meets users' needs, departmental and wider government objectives.
- The preferred option maximises value for money.

- The preferred option is affordable over its full duration and is supported by the relevant internal and external stakeholders.
- The correct tendering process has been followed and the procuring entity has complied with all the relevant procurement guidelines and regulations.
- The preferred partner is capable of delivering the contract.
- The contract reflects standard 'tram-line' terms (including appropriate risk transfer).
- Risks have been comprehensively identified, assessed, financially evaluated (where appropriate) and appropriately allocated.
- The organisation is 'ready' to implement the contract.
- Sound arrangements are in place to lead, manage, implement, monitor and evaluate the project.

In summary, the conclusions about strategic fit, value for money, selection of preferred service provider, affordability and achievability must be supported by rigorous analyses and sound underpinning evidence. Appendix 2 indicates the issues which are typically addressed in a FBC.

Level of detail for SOCs

A SOC will generally address the same issues as an OBC but at a higher level and in far less detail. The main focus is on strategic issues and identification of options for detailed assessment at a later stage. Too much detailed assessment at the SOC stage may serve to cloud judgements about the merits and demerits of the available options in delivering the project objectives. The structure and content of all three levels of business case is compared in Appendix 2.

There are no hard-and-fast rules for the length of the document. Much will depend on whether or not the project is novel, inherently risky or complex. One indicator of complexity is the number of stakeholders who have an interest in the project. A SOC for a single-organisation procurement will generally contain less detail than a multi-agency procurement.

Availability of information, personnel and other resources will also influence the length of the document. A pragmatic approach should be adopted. If the information is available, this should be used subject to any time constraints on the decision-making process. SOCs produced to date for construction schemes range from 15 to 60 pages. There are examples of SOCs for IM&T projects which are less than ten pages long.

The SOC should be driven by its fundamental purpose and the information which is required by the decision makers at this stage of the process, rather than pre-occupation with size. Size does not matter in this case.

The SOC should be viewed as a scoping and planning document, designed to:

- establish the strategic context and need for the project
- identify key dependencies between the project and other projects in the portfolio (including their main stakeholders)
- identify a wide range of viable options for meeting the service objectives
- appraise the relative efficacy of the options and their affordability and, where feasible, identify a short list for more rigorous assessment at the OBC stage
- identify the critical success factors for developing and implementing the project with emphasis on risk management and benefit realisation
- identify what further work needs to be undertaken to inform the development of the OBC and the procurement process.

Once completed and agreed, the SOC represents an important milestone. Assuming the project is recommended to be continued, the SOC provides direction to the project sponsors on how best to develop and implement it. Although it may be perceived as an extra stage in the business planning process, the work done at this stage would, in any event, need to be conducted as part of the development of the OBC. **The SOC aids and feeds directly into the OBC, thereby expediting the business case and procurement process**.

A SOC should contain the five components that characterise all soundly developed business cases, albeit in less detail than is expected from OBCs and FBCs.

Much of the material in a SOC will focus disproportionately on the strategic case, economic case and project management case. Details about the commercial case generally do not become available until after the project has been advertised and tenders have been submitted (i.e. the post-OBC stage). Nevertheless, early thought needs to be given to the nature of the deal and the desired contract. The feasibility of the proposed deal can subsequently be investigated once the project has been advertised.

Outcomes from SOC process

The possible outcomes from the work undertaken at the SOC stage are:

- abandon the project (perhaps on grounds of affordability and/or inability to manage the risks successfully)

- redefine the project to make it more manageable and improve the likelihood of a successful outcome
- undertake a pilot or prototype and use the results of this experience to inform how best to proceed with the project
- continue with the project as originally conceived with a set of broad recommendations on how to proceed, including a short list of options for more rigorous assessment at the OBC stage. In general, this will not include identification of a preferred option since the analysis undertaken as part of a SOC will not be sufficiently robust to support an unequivocal conclusion.

SOCs should be produced by a multidisciplinary team, drawing on the appropriate skills and involving representation from key stakeholders. Workshops and focused meetings should be built into the project timetable.

The 'five-case model' (i.e. strategic case, economic case, financial case, commercial case and project management case) should be adopted for structuring SOCs. However, the main emphasis should be on 'strategic issues' and a wide range of options for meeting the project objectives (i.e. the 'strategic case' and 'economic case'). These are defined in the main report.

Sound project management arrangements should be developed from the inception of all projects before scarce public resources are committed to them. Roles, responsibilities, reporting and accountability should be clearly defined. Close attention should be paid to critical success factors from the outset. This should include involvement of end-users, benefit realisation, risk management, communication, training, change management and resources for life-cycle project management.

Finally, it should be stressed that SOCs do **not** impose additional cost or effort on project sponsors and their stakeholders. On the contrary, timescales are shortened, or at least not lengthened, because much of the work done as part of the SOC would, in any event, need to be conducted as part of the development of the OBC. The earlier focus on defining the project parameters and critical success factors also lead to more robust thinking, improved project design and increases the likelihood of successful project implementation (including shorter approval loops).

SOCs constitute best practice. Given the benefits they offer (at no additional cost), it is recommended that policy makers, business planners and other managers adopt SOCs as part of their normal business planning and procurement process.

Unlike OBCs and FBCs, SOCs do not require formal approval from HM Treasury and other bodies normally involved in the approval process. However, project sponsors will find it advantageous to share completed SOCs with these bodies and other stakeholders (local, regional and national) to engage them early and improve their understanding of their proposals before they are formally submitted for approval. This helps to expedite the approval and procurement process.

The procurement cycle and its fit with the business case process

A business case, if approved, will invariably result in a procurement and the award of a contract to the chosen service provider(s). This section clarifies the relationship between the business case and procurement processes. The procurement cycle is characterised by three distinct phases, each of which is informed by the business case process:

- **Phase 1:** Planning and preparing to meet the business need.
- **Phase 2:** Purchasing the solution.
- **Phase 3:** Performing the contract.

We will discuss each of these three stages briefly in turn. Chapter 9 provides further details on these stages, including guidance on how to manage the procurement process to secure the desired outcome. Figure 2.2 shows the relationship between the procurement cycle and the business case process. For ease of presentation, we assume the project will be privately financed.

Planning and preparation

To state the obvious, a carefully planned procurement exercise is more likely to yield a good, value-for-money deal than an ill-thought-through exercise. The adage 'poor planning produces poor performance' must be heeded.

It is during this stage that the SOC and OBC are produced. This will culminate in the approval of the OBC. Departments are required to obtain approval for their OBC *before* advertising the project.

By the end of this stage, the following milestones will have been established:

- production of a project initiation document
- appointment of the project team and advisers
- clear definition of the objectives and scope of the project
- clear definition of the business need in terms of outputs and outcomes
- identification of the preferred option
- development of a public sector comparator (PSC) (i.e. a description of the public sector's solution for meeting the project objectives, including an estimate of the costs, benefits and risks associated with this solution)

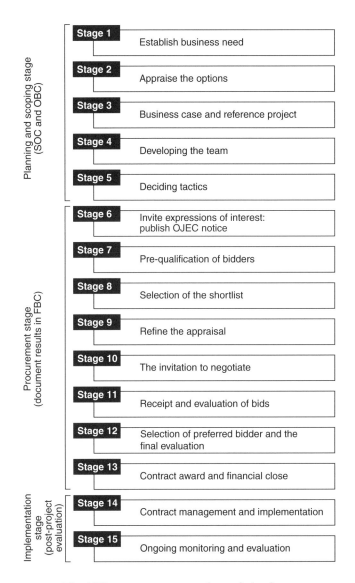

Figure 2.2: The PFI procurement cycle and the business case process.

- completion of market sounding activities
- production of the procurement strategy and timetable
- clear position on the desired partnership, risk allocation, payment mechanism, performance regime and other commercial issues
- development of OJEC notice
- approval of the OBC
- completing all necessary consultations, including statutory requirements such as planning permission in the case of building proposals

- development of full output-based specification, pre-qualification questionnaires, evaluation criteria and tender evaluation model.

Much of this work will have been undertaken as part of the SOC and
OBC. The main exception is development of full output-based specification,
pre-qualification questionnaires, evaluation criteria and tender evaluation
model. These documents can be prepared in parallel with the approval of
the OBC.

The amount of work done during the planning and preparation phase
will have a significant bearing on the length of the procurement process.
If all the above requirements are satisfied prior to OJEC or before the end
of the 37 days that need to be allowed for lodging the OJEC notice, the
solution can normally be procured within 12 months.

Purchasing the solution

It is during this phase that the FBC is developed. This phase is characterised
by the following procurement activities:

- issue OJEC notice
- pre-qualification of bidders
- selection of the short list
- invitation to negotiate contract schedules and terms
- receipt and evaluation of bids
- produce FBC
- selection of preferred bidder and the final evaluation
- contract award and financial close.

Before contract award and financial close, a FBC should be produced to
document the results of the procurement process and the selection of the
preferred bidder (including reserve bidder, if this route is chosen). The FBC
must demonstrate that the proposed deal satisfies all approval requirements
laid down by the sponsor's management board, HM Treasury and other
relevant approval bodies (*see* Chapter 10 for more details).

Perform the contract

This phase is characterised by the following key activities:

- implement the contract
- conduct post-implementation activities

- performance monitoring
- ongoing contract management and review
- conduct formal post-project evaluations.

It is important for the post-implementation mechanisms to be agreed with the service provider(s). Both the procuring organisation and the service provider(s) will need to appoint dedicated project managers. The contract should be managed according to PRINCE project management principles.

Concluding remarks

The key points from this chapter may be summarised as follows:

- Capital investment represents an ongoing and iterative process rather than a discrete, one-off activity.
- There are six broad stages in the process – generation of proposals, initial screen, project definition and analysis, selection, implementation and post-implementation review.
- Each stage in the process needs to be underpinned with appropriate information, analysis and documentation.
- Three levels of analyses and types of business cases are required – SOCs, OBCs and FBCs.
- Each of these types of case maps onto the 'five-case model', albeit in different levels of detail.
- The business case process should be approached positively. It should not be viewed as a series of hoops which are required to obtain approval to proceed with the investment.
- A business case, if approved, will invariably result in a procurement and the award of a contract.
- The procurement cycle has three main stages which mirror the business case process. The three stages are planning and preparing to meet the business need, purchasing the solution and performing the contract.
- The project should not be advertised until the necessary approvals have been secured at the OBC stage.

PART TWO

Unpacking the 'five-case model'

CHAPTER THREE

The strategic case

This chapter explains the role of the strategic case in the capital investment decision-making process. It provides guidance on how to make the case for change, identify strategic drivers within the organisation's operating environment, formulate investment objectives, and lay the foundation for identification and assessment of options to satisfy the business need. Individuals putting forward investment proposals should ensure the project is in line with the organisation's strategic objectives.

Introduction

The meaning of the word 'strategy' derives from the Greek 'art of war' and is open to a number of interpretations. In today's management parlance, it is essentially involved with forward planning and competitive edge, hence consideration of the following key themes:

- Where are we now? *The existing situation.*
- Where do we want to be? *The strategic direction and vision.*
- How do we get there? *The required actions.*

Early consideration should be given to the extent to which the organisation's business strategies should be shared with others, both within and outside the organisation. The prevailing management theory is that it should be shared; but in practice, this rarely seems to go beyond communicating strategic vision and goals in order to preserve the competitive edge. Perhaps the Duke of Wellington had it all summed up on the battlefield of Waterloo. When asked by General Sir Thomas Picton if he would take his soldiers into his confidence, he replied, 'If I thought my hair knew what my brain was thinking, I'd shave it off and wear a wig.'

The definition of the strategic context and formulation of the strategic case has a major bearing on the success or otherwise of the project. The scope of the strategic case is reproduced in Box 3.1 for ease of reference. We will now discuss these issues in turn.

Box 3.1: The scope of the strategic case

Strategic context
Organisational overview
Existing business strategies

The case for change – strategic needs
Investment objectives
Existing arrangements
Business needs – current and future
Potential scope and service requirements
Benefits criteria
Strategic risks
Constraints and dependencies

Strategic context

Key to the successful preparation of the strategic case is the concept of holistic fit, whereby all parts of the organisation's activities fit together to provide a value which is greater than the sum of its parts.

Drawing on the organisation's corporate and business plans, the strategic context for the proposal should be clearly defined. It should address issues such as:

- What is the remit of the organisation?
- How is demand for its services likely to change over the next three to five years?
- What are its strategic objectives over this period?
- How well-placed is the organisation to achieve its remit and objectives?
- Is the organisation aware of its strengths, weaknesses, opportunities and threats?
- Are its existing business strategies still valid?
- What value will the proposed investment add to where the organisation would like to be in the medium to long term?

In summary, this section of the strategic case should provide the backcloth within which the proposed investment falls, and help to demonstrate business fit and synergy with other parts of the organisation's business strategies.

Organisational overview

If the case is to be reviewed and approved by an external body, it will often prove beneficial to provide a profile of the organisation. In the private sector, this is likely to be the case for companies seeking approval from their parent (or holding) company. In the public sector, it is likely to be the case for departments seeking approval from HM Treasury, or Executive Agencies from their parent departments.

Organisations now have a habit of changing and restructuring at an alarming rate; so much so that in five to ten years' time, few managers will be able to remember, with any real clarity, what their organisations were like. It will prove invaluable, therefore, to have recorded a snapshot of the organisation.

This section should provide a brief profile of the organisation, a statement of what it is seeking to achieve, and the level and nature of the resources currently at its disposal. The key areas of interest will include:

- the mission of the organisation
- its strategic goals, business aims and service objectives
- its current activities and services, including key stakeholders and customers
- its organisational structure, staff complement, turnover and geographical position
- existing funding arrangements.

Existing business strategies

The justification for incurring expenditure should be considered in the context of relevant government, corporate business plans and strategies.

At any point in time, the organisation will have a number of key business strategies in place to support and deliver its organisational goals. Examples of such strategies range from the use of information services (IS) and information technology (IT) to human resources (HR) and change management.

In some instances, these may relate to the strategies of other organisations. They may include the strategies of the parent company in the case of private sector companies, and those of the parent department or government policies in the public sector.

This section should explain how the proposed investment fits within, supports and promotes an agreed strategy, programme or project. In particular, it will outline how the proposal supports the business goals, strategic objectives and plans of the organisation.

Consider the following example. Future expenditure on the provision of Electronic Patient Records (EPRs) within the NHS will further the NHS business strategy (*The NHS Plan*) and its underpinning Information Services Strategy (*Information for Health*) by helping to achieve the strategic objectives shown in Box 3.2.

Box 3.2: Information for health strategic objectives

For clinical professionals
● Provision of reliable and rapid access to patient information
● On-line access to local and national evidence on treatment
● Access to effective information

For patients
● Access to accredited independent information
● Provision of on-line access to services and specialists

For the public
● Fast and convenient access to accredited information
● Involvement in health service policy

For managers and planners
● Availability of accurate information for planning purposes

The case for change

The purpose of this section of the strategic case is to explain the need for the investment. This may range from the replacement of an existing asset to the provision of a new service, incorporating elements of business process re-engineering.

This section should address the following questions:

● What are the reasons for any proposed investment?
● What is wrong with the status quo?
● What is the affordability envelope for any resulting investment?

Investment (or project) objectives

The investment objectives for the project should be clearly related to the underlying policies and strategies of the organisation. They should be made SMART – **S**pecific, **M**easurable, **A**chievable, **R**elevant and **T**ime-constrained. This helps to facilitate generation and assessment of options, as well as post-implementation review.

Investment objectives for the service to be provided should be customer-focused and distinguished from the means of provision. In other words, they should focus on what needs to be achieved rather than on how it is to be achieved. They should not be so narrowly defined as to exclude important options. Conversely, they must not be too broad so as to cause unnecessary work at the option appraisal stage (HM Treasury, 1997).

The setting of robust investment objectives is an iterative process: appraisal may itself help to clarify, justify, question or change the investment objectives. Specialist help should be sought to ensure objectives are defined at the right level and in SMART terms. Generally, investment objectives will be predicated upon one or all of the following themes:

- to provide further economies in the provision of an existing service(s)
- to improve business effectiveness and quality in terms of the required outcomes
- to improve efficiencies in the throughput of services
- to meet statutory requirements and obligations
- to meet policy changes (e.g. government policy in the case of the public sector)
- to deliver new business and operational targets.

Existing arrangements and business needs

The need for further investment will be unclear if the existing arrangements underpinning the business activity or service under review are not clearly defined. The review of how services are currently organised and delivered will throw up potential areas for improvement. There may also be changes in demand, both current and future, which will have a bearing on business needs. A robust case for the proposed investment is vital, if it is not to be viewed as simply 'a nice thing to do'.

This section of the strategic case should assess the adequacy or otherwise of existing arrangements – Where are we now? – in relation to the desired arrangements – Where do we want to be? – as depicted and described in the investment objectives for the proposal. The difference between the two is the business gap that needs to be filled.

In this context, it should be noted that the existing arrangements for the provision of a required service could be non-existent at present; so, in effect, the organisation requires a new service starting from scratch. But in most cases, it will generally be necessary to include:

- confirmation of the continued need for the business operations, including supporting evidence
- projections of the nature and level of demand for the business operations
- deficiencies of current service provision
- a summary of users' requirements, clearly distinguishing new from existing requirements.

A useful technique for populating this section of the business case is to complete the following template:

Investment objective (clear statement):

Existing arrangement (brief description):

Related business need (What's wrong with the status quo, including the gap that needs to be filled as a consequence?)

An example of this in respect of EPRs for the NHS might be as follows:

Investment objective:
To support the delivery of improved patient services through the provision of electronically held patient information by July 2002, in accordance with *The NHS Plan* published in July 2000.

Existing arrangement (brief description):
Patient records are presently held manually in most instances within the NHS, in accordance with the statutory obligations and the basic needs of clinicians within the acute sector and general practitioners within the primary care sector.

Related business need (What's wrong with the status quo, including the gap that needs to be filled as a consequence?):
The manual recording of patients' history within a paper-based system is resource-intensive and does not provide the most cost-effective and efficient means of recording data.

   Moreover, it does not provide healthcare professionals with an up-to-date, readily accessible record of a patient's medical history from which to prescribe the highest possible standard and quality of treatment, when and where it is needed. And from the patients' perspective,

---

> it does not provide individuals with immediate access to reliable infor-
> mation from which to improve their knowledge of, and involvement
> in, their own treatment in accordance with NHS policy objectives.

Potential scope and key service requirements

In response to the investment objectives and business needs, this section
of the case describes the resultant service gap or potential scope in relation
to the required services. Early resolution of the scope of the investment
is fundamental to the successful and timely completion of the business
case, since all options subsequently appraised (in the economic case) will fall
(or perhaps should fall) within the overall parameters of the agreed scope.

All too often, though, this vital choice is left unresolved until the last
moment. The end result is uncertainty on the part of the project team,
indecision on the part of management and creeping scope on the part of the
project.

In practice, it will prove advantageous to outline the potential scope and
associated requirement for services in relation to their core (minimum),
desirable (intermediate) and optional (maximum) need and functionality.

A useful technique for populating this section of the business case is to
complete the following template:

Business scope	Service requirements
Core (minimum requirement)	Core (minimum requirement)
Desirable (intermediate requirement)	Desirable (intermediate requirement)
Optional (maximum requirement)	Optional (maximum requirement)

An example of business scope and service requirements in respect of EPRs
for the NHS is shown in Table 3.1.

Key benefits criteria

Alongside the investment objectives agreed for the project, benefit criteria
should be derived to provide a basis for selecting and evaluating options
(*see* Economic case in Chapter 4 for more detail).

Table 3.1: An example of business scope and service requirements

Business scope	Service requirements
Core (minimum requirement) • Patient demographics including: NHS number; name and address; screening information; vaccination and immunisation status; prescription exemption data	Core (minimum requirement) • Access to service on a web browser for the acute sector
Desirable (intermediate requirement) • In addition to the core scope, information on current medications, alerts and allergies, and blood groups	Desirable (intermediate requirement) • In addition to the core service, a facility for on-line access to current prescribing alerts and other basic clinical information within the acute sector
Optional (maximum requirement) • In addition to the core and desirable scope, information on ongoing conditions	Optional (maximum requirement) • In addition to the core and desirable services, on-line access to patient records held within the primary care sector

The benefits criteria must be developed by the parties affected directly by the proposal, usually the main stakeholders and customers (or users). A useful framework for capturing the benefits associated with each investment objective is shown in Table 3.2.

Table 3.2: Framework for identifying benefits

Class	Relative value	Relative time-scale	General type
Strategic (business-related) e.g. future proofing	High	Long-term	Qualitative Indirect/direct – non-cash-releasing
Operational (management-related) e.g. improved quality and efficiency	Medium	Medium-term	Mixture Direct Cash-releasing Non-cash-releasing
Job (task-related) e.g. reduced costs and staff savings	Low	Short-term	Quantitative Direct Cash-releasing Non-cash-releasing

Table 3.3: Benefit criteria of EPRs for the NHS

Investment objective	Related benefits criteria	Weight
Objective 1 • to support the delivery of improved patient services by	Patients and the public • Improved healthcare through provision of better, more timely information • Improved access through direct (one-stop) booking of multiple appointments Clinicians • More appropriate prescribing • Ability to compare patients' notes Managers and administrators • Better co-ordination of discharge arrangements	50%
Objective 2 • to support the more flexible management of services by	Patients and the public • Reductions in waiting times • Reductions in cancelled admissions and appointments Clinicians • More effective and efficient use of clinicians' time • Ability to respond quicker and more flexibly to changing demands Managers and administrators • More effective team-working • Improved monitoring and reporting arrangements	30%
Objective 3		10%
Objective 4		10%

Assessing the potential benefits associated with individual investment objectives in this way helps:

- to indicate the relative value, and thus individual weight or priority, of the investment objectives. This is essential for rank, weighting and scoring the options (*see* Chapter 4, Economic case)
- to pinpoint the main beneficiaries of the scheme. Those pertaining to the organisation and their customers are referred to as direct benefits; those to other stakeholders and organisations as indirect benefits. The party who

benefits most from the investment might not always be the party con-
tributing to the bulk of the costs

- to ascertain whether benefits can be quantified financially (cash-releasing
  and non-cash-releasing), or quantified but not in financial terms (quanti-
  fiables – non-£); or whether benefits cannot be quantified (qualitative
  benefits). This analysis will help to indicate early on whether the proposal is affordable.

It is important for this section of the case to record the benefit criteria
(by stakeholder group) for each investment objective, together with an overview of who was involved in the identification and prioritisation process.

An example of this in respect of EPRs for the NHS is given in Table 3.3.
This example is based on output from a workshop which involved patients
(users), clinician (technical) and health service managers (business).

Key strategic risks

Delivering projects or investments to the required quality (in terms of
the desired business outcomes and service outputs), to cost and within the
required time-frame is largely about the management of associated risks.
It is, therefore, essential to identify the risks associated with the investment
as early as possible.

At this stage, emphasis should be placed on the 20% of risks that potentially will account for 80% of the value of risk. Risk may be identified in
three broad categories (*see* Table 3.4). We provide a more complete framework for identifying, assessing and apportioning risks in Chapter 8:

Table 3.4: Broad categories of risks

Risk categories	Description
Business risks	These are often referred to as *strategic* risks They remain with the business or organisation regardless of how the service is provided
Service risks	These risks are associated with the design, build, financial and operational phases of services They can often be shared with business partners and potentially transferred to the service provider
External environmental risks	These risks affect all organisations within the economy

Table 3.5: Illustration of a high-level risk management strategy

Key categories	Main approach to risk management
Business risks	
• Inadequate scoping of the project	Specification and requirements to be compiled in conjunction with business partners, main customers and stakeholders
• Business failure	Resultant services to be periodically reviewed in conjunction with business strategy and plans
• Inability to cope with required business change	Change control mechanisms to be put in place
• Poor image and reputation	Customer-satisfaction surveys as part of agreed marketing and communications strategy
Service risks	
• Shortage of required skills	Competencies and capability audit to be undertaken. Human resource plans adjusted accordingly
• Poor design and build	Adoption of robust method and inclusion of business, technical and user input
• Lack of supply-side capability and capacity	Market soundings and intelligence gathering of potential suppliers
• Poor project management	Adoption of project management methodology
• Increased costs and reduced benefits	Robust contract management strategy and benefit realisation plan during operational phase
External environmental risks	
• Changes in secondary legislation (e.g. Health and Safety and VAT)	Transfer to the service provider as part of the contract
• Higher-than-expected rates of inflation	Contingency within cost estimates, if over the general level of inflation

The main risks associated with the project during its design, build and operational phases should be detailed here, together with an initial assessment of how they will be managed. The aim is to demonstrate that the main risks can be managed so as to ensure that the project is ultimately a success. An illustration of a high-level risk management strategy at this stage for a project might be as shown in Table 3.5.

Key constraints and dependencies

All investments will be subject to constraints and things that may need to happen outside the immediate sphere of the project (dependencies) to

Table 3.6: Key constraints and dependencies associated with the NHS's EPR programme

Constraints	Dependencies
• Financial ceilings in terms of affordability • Technical feasibility of the proposed solution • The ability of the organisation to absorb the degree of required change • Agreed changes in organisational policy, e.g. government policy in the case of public sector organisations	• The successful delivery of other projects within the strategy and programme • The agreement and approval of key stakeholders and customers • The willingness of stakeholders and customers to engage in a pilot approach to the implementation of the solution

ensure that it is a success. In other words, constraints impose restrictions on what can be done and/or achieved, whereas dependencies are the actions or products which must be in place in order to deliver the outcome in question.

Too often, these issues are ignored, with disastrous consequences. For example, the success of the Millennium Dome project was dependent largely on:

• putting in place the infrastructure for local transport
• a given level of sponsorship (£) from the private sector
• 12 million visitors.

The primary constraint was the agreed level of funding from the National Lottery. In the event, it proved difficult to travel to and from the Dome and the project failed to attract the required level of sponsorship and number of visitors. Consequently, the Millennium Dome project was technically bankrupt and had to be bailed out by further, unanticipated, tranches of funding.

This section of the case should summarise briefly the key constraints and dependencies associated with the case.

By way of illustration, in the case of the NHS's EPR programme these might include the examples shown in Table 3.6.

An important point to remember is that any constraints must be real. Arbitary time-scales and cost ceilings should be avoided, unless the budget for the service has been fixed at the highest level within the organisation and the deadline agreed is on a critical path for the organisation.

Conclusion

The key points from this chapter may be summarised as follows:

- Remember throughout that the principal goals in the preparation of this section are: first, to make the case for change by evidencing business need and strategic fit; and second, to provide the resultant scope for subsequent analysis in the economic case section.
- Be absolutely clear on the investment or project objectives for your proposal and make sure they are SMART, so all relevant options can be identified and subsequently appraised. Explain how these objectives support the wider business and service objectives of the organisation.
- For each investment objective, related business need and associated service stream, list the associated benefits by key stakeholder group, type of benefit, potential value and time-scale.
- Ensure all key risks are identified.
- Identify the key constraints and dependencies associated with the project.

CHAPTER FOUR

The economic case

This chapter explains the role of the economic case in the capital investment decision-making process. In line with the purpose of the economic case, our main focus is on providing guidance, tips and best practice to help decision makers optimise value for money from scarce public resources. We provide a novel approach, 'the options framework', to ensure a wide range of options is considered and rigorously evaluated. We also emphasise the need for managers to pay greater attention to 'implementation options', particularly the adoption of 'incremental' and 'modular' approaches as a means of mitigating the risks associated with novel and complex projects. Supporting tools and techniques for this chapter are provided in Chapter 8.

Introduction

Within the neo-classical economics paradigm, economics is generally defined in terms of allocation of scarce resources between competing ends. The task facing the decision maker is to select the course of action that will maximise the use of resources and deliver the highest ratio of benefits to costs. In the context of public sector investments, this boils down to maximising value for money.

The purpose of the economic case is:

- to revisit the investment objectives for the proposal and determine the critical success factors (CSFs) for the project
- to consider the widest possible range of relevant options (the long list)
- to identify, quantify and value the costs, benefits, risks and uncertainties of all short-listed options on a comparable basis
- to weigh up the uncertainties associated with each short-listed option (sensitivity analysis)
- to assess the results from the various analyses and recommend the preferred way forward.

The scope of the economic case is reproduced in Box 4.1. Each of these sections is discussed in turn. Supporting tools and techniques are presented in Chapter 8 for those readers who need to brush up on investment appraisal principles.

Box 4.1: The scope of the economic case

Critical success factors

Long-listed options
Potential business scopes
Potential service and technical solutions
Potential methods of service delivery
Potential implementation period
Potential methods of funding

The preferred way forward

Short-listed options
Baseline – status quo; do minimum
The public sector comparator (PSC)
Other short-listed options

Economic appraisals
NPC/NPV findings
Benefits appraisal
Risks assessment
Sensitivity analysis

The preferred option

Selecting critical success factors (CSFs)

An early task to address before selection and assessment of options is identification of CSFs for the project. These are the criteria against which the options identified within the economic case must be evaluated to identify the option that provides optimal fit and returns.

In practice, the main CSFs for the project will comprise of a combination of the investment objectives for the project and the salient attributes of the 'five-case model' itself. The key thing to remember is that the identification and choice of CSFs is critical to the evaluation of long-listed options. It follows, therefore, that they must be selected with great care and be subject to agreement by the parties involved in the preparation of the case.

Table 4.1: Critical success factors for a proposed investment

Key critical success factors	Broad description
Strategic fit and business needs (the strategic case)	How well the option: • meets agreed investment objectives, related business needs and service requirements. This will include quality of service and the need for flexibility in response to future business change • provides holistic fit and synergy with other key elements and parts of the organisation's business strategies
Potential VFM (the economic case)	How well the option: • maximises the return on the required investment (benefits optimisation) in terms of economy, efficiency and effectiveness • minimises associated risks
Supply-side capacity and capability (the commercial case)	How well the option: • matches the ability of service providers and suppliers to deliver the required levels of service and functionality • appeals to suppliers
Potential affordability (the financial case)	How well the option: • meets the source and pattern of available funding • matches other financial constraints
Potential achievability (the project management case)	How well the option: • is likely to be delivered in view of the organisation's ability to assimilate, adapt and respond to the level of required change • satisfies the level of available skills which are required to deliver the project successfully

The CSFs for a proposed investment will inevitably vary from case to case, both in terms of content and relative importance. They are derived from the investment objectives and will typically address the five broad areas shown in Table 4.1.

Long-listed options

The main options or alternative ways of meeting the business needs and service requirements specified in the strategic case should be considered.

In the case of public sector organisations, HM Treasury's 'Green Book' suggests in the order of a dozen main options. This is known as the long list.

When selecting options for the long-list, it is important to select only those which satisfy the project's investment objectives and meet the critical success factors for the project. Best practice suggests that options should be generated by working parties (brainstorming exercises), comprised of senior managers (business input), stakeholders (user input) and specialists (technical input).

However, there is a tendency for the long-list to be drawn from a selection of preconceived ideas. At best this leads to suboptimal investments and, at worst, to considerable delays in the approval of expenditure proposals.

Box 4.2: What **not** to do!

We once observed a group of executives brainstorming and selecting options for subsequent analysis. Eleven people sat in the board room. Eleven options emerged – one from each attendee.

After considerable discussion the preferred way forward emerged. Surprise, surprise, it had been put forward by the chief executive!

The key purpose of this section of the case is to demonstrate that consideration has been given to the widest possible range of options prior to the selection of a short-list for full analysis. The process by which options have been sifted should be made clear, including reasons for rejection. As a matter of course, it is important to include the 'do nothing' or 'do minimum' option – the minimum level of investment required to satisfy the core requirement. This should be retained as a baseline option.

Expenditure should not be regarded as unavoidable, because it replaces worn out services or assets. It may be preferable, for example, to close or outsource an operation or service – or to modify it to provide a different level of service – and to use the resources that are released in another way.

Sometimes, options will appear to be ruled out by legal, financial or political constraints. Although undue time and effort should not be spent on appraising these options, it is important to ensure the constraints in question are not artificially imposed.

Box 4.3: Health warning – public sector organisations

In the case of public sector organisations, public expenditure constraints should not restrict the initial choice of options for consideration.

> Controls or targets set in the interests of greater efficiency and account-
> ability are not intended to limit the range of possible solutions.
> If public expenditure controls and targets lead to the rejection of the
> most cost-effective option this should be brought out in the appraisal.
>
> *Source*: HM Treasury 'Green Book' (1997)

An option may affect, or be affected by, other expenditure. Where a number of expenditures are linked and the costs and benefits are mutually dependent, the programme must be justified in its entirety. Proposals of this nature should be considered as a single option within the long-list.

Conversely, it should not be taken for granted that every project in a programme is justified in its own right. In some cases, proposals will need to be split into separate options, since what may appear to be a good option might include elements which provide suboptimal value. Where possible, the unattractive elements should be stripped out.

The 'Treasury Green Book' indicates that the long list should consider:

- the alternatives for the timing or phasing of expenditure
- alternative methods of funding or financing
- different methods of service provision.

Each option in the long list should be subjected to SWOT analysis: an assessment of its relative **S**trengths and **W**eaknesses (against internal factors) and **O**pportunities and **T**hreats (against external factors). Generally, it will prove helpful to capture this information in the format shown in Table 4.2. This example is based on a business need for a prison inmate information service.

The options framework

Despite a plethora of guidance on the importance of the long-list and assembling a wide range of possible options for analysis at the outset, projects often fail to consider all the available choices. This results in either delayed approval for the case or suboptimal investment.

To help overcome these difficulties, we have devised the 'options framework', which seeks to provide a simple and straightforward approach to the identification of a broad range of relevant options for investment.

The framework has been thoroughly tested in a number of significant procurements within the public sector and has proved particularly useful in

Table 4.2: Format for capturing information for a SWOT analysis (a case study)

Description Option 1 – 'Do nothing'	This option assumes that the prison service would continue to maintain its existing prisoner inmate systems. Current systems would not therefore be replaced, expanded or upgraded as they became technically obsolete.
	Current automated systems include: prisoner records, petty cash, tuck shop, medical records, recreational activities, etc.
	Manual paper-based systems include: movement and absences, court scheduling, request and complaints, sentence calculation, prisoner property, etc.
Main advantages	The main advantages of this option are: • that it would incur no additional expenditure beyond the straightforward maintenance of existing systems • that it would incur no additional risks in terms of service provision
Main disadvantages	The main disadvantages of this option are: • that it would not address the Prison Service's urgent requirement for change in respect of existing and future services • that it would not meet the prison's future statutory obligations • that it would not provide the considerable business and service benefits which could accrue through the improved use of IS/IT
Conclusion	This option (do nothing) is not a feasible or realistic option in existing circumstances. It would not meet the prison's investment objectives to act in accordance with statutory obligations, to support the delivery of improved prisoner care or to make the best use of prison resources
	It has, therefore, been discounted for further consideration. The 'do minimum' option (the next level up) becomes the baseline for further consideration

getting senior management signed-up and committed to the preferred way forward early on in the business planning process.

The framework provides a systematic approach to, first, the identification of a broad range of relevant options and, second, identification of a preferred option within each of the key parameters considered.

The hierarchy – or key categories – for the selection of options is shown in Table 4.3.

The process for pinpointing the preferred way forward is straightforward and undertaken as follows:

- **Step 1:** The options in the first category – potential scope – are identified and the preferred choice selected.
- **Step 2:** The options in the second category – service solutions – for delivering the preferred choice in the first category are selected and the preferred choice selected.

Table 4.3: Overview: the options framework

Category of choice	Brief description
Scoping options	The **what** (levels of outcomes) in terms of the **why** (coverage of investment objectives and business needs) and the **where** (geographical, functional and service spread): these relate to business needs and the combinations for underpinning services, e.g. levels of coverage and functionality within the organisation
Technical options	The **what** in terms of the **how**: these relate to the composition and technical attributes of potential solutions, e.g. automation as opposed to paper-based solutions within the organisation
Service delivery options	The **what** in terms of the **who**: these relate to the potential methods of delivery, e.g. doing it in partnership with other organisations – private or public – or doing it on a single organisational basis
Implementation options	The **what** in terms of the **when**: these relate to the timing and phasing of options, e.g. big bang and full implementation of the total package as opposed to 'incremental' and 'modular' approaches.
Funding options	The **what** in terms of available methods of **funding** and finance, e.g. exchequer funding as opposed to leasing, private finance and other forms of funding

- **Step 3:** The process is carried on through the remaining categories within the hierarchy. Ultimately, the preferred way forward emerges for further consideration during the short-listing stage.

It is important to note that while the hierarchy is comprehensive and will meet the needs of most organisations, it will require tailoring to the particular circumstances of the organisation. For example, organisations may wish to explore the options available in terms of procurements (collaborative, single or national, regional and local) as part of the framework.

Table 4.4: Summary of The Prison Service's strategic case

Strategic overview	The **business strategy** of the prison service is comprised of a number of **work programmes**, one of which seeks to satisfy the following **strategic objective**: • to provide prison staff with information and systems they require to provide an effective, efficient and professional service to prisoners, the public and wider criminal justice community
Business needs and service gaps	In relation to the above objective, the prison service has identified the following problems: • major functional gaps and inefficiencies caused by staff not having ready access to supporting IS/IT • service gaps in the provision of up-to-date and accurate information • the duplication of information The prison service requires a business solution which will address these service gaps
Investment objectives	These are: • to provide staff with IS/IT by 2005 • to provide prisoners, their families and the Department of the Interior with accurate and up-to-date information; • to achieve efficiency savings of 10% pa within the next three years These objectives were scoped at the outset and have been firmed-up following a detailed study of need
Potential scope and service requirements	Meeting all operational needs through the introduction of an Electronic Prisoner Record, as supported by the prison service's IS/IT strategy

Case study background

The information in Table 4.4 emerges from an analysis of the prison service's strategic case. We will build on this information to illustrate the options framework and the other elements of the economic case.

Scoping options

The broad scope of the investment should emerge from the strategic case. It is now time to pin this down in more precise terms. What is the coverage of the investment in terms of business functions, departmental/geographical spread and service requirements? What is in, what is out?

The range of potential scopes will vary depending on:

- how well the business needs and required services have already been analysed and defined within the organisation's business strategies, including supporting information services
- users' requirements
- the complexity of the project and the risks inherent in it
- the degree of change required.

This can range from the automation of existing processes (improved economy), to their improvement through redesign (improved efficiency) and, ultimately, transformation through business process re-engineering (improved effectiveness). The model in Table 4.5 defines five potential degrees of change within an organisation through the improved penetration of IT.

Table 4.5: Five potential degrees of change within an organisation

Level of change	Impact
1 Localise exploitation	Automation of discrete activities
2 Internal integration	Automation and integration of all organisational activities
3 Business process redesign	Automation and streamlining of organisational activities
4 Business network redesign	Automation and communication with external customers and stakeholders
5 Business scope redefinition	Altering fundamentally the mission, purpose and outputs of the organisation

Business planners will need to think through all the relevant issues for themselves in the context of their own organisation's unique set of circumstances. Some business areas and functions might be excluded for strategic and operational reasons. Others might be included to reap economies of scale.

Table 4.6: Choice of services in relation to business needs

Scoping options (1)	Description of options and extent to which business needs are met
1.1 Do nothing	Status quo – needs not met at all
1.2 Do minimum	Minimal investment – replacement of systems as required. Marginal improvement
1.3 Electronic Prison Records plus minimum scope	Provision of basic Electronic Prisoner Record plus: • core, existing operational services only • main location only • core service streams • some processes only Significant improvement but does not satisfy all the investment objectives
1.4 Electronic Prison Records plus intermediate scope	Provision of basic Electronic Prisoner Record plus: • coverage of core and new operational services • two prison locations, including main • immediate range of service streams • all existing processes Meets all the investment objectives and CSFs for the project at the lowest possible risk to the prison service
1.5 Electronic Prison Records plus maximum scope	Provision of basic Electronic Prisoner Record plus: • coverage of all operational services • all prison locations • full range of service streams • all existing and new processes Meets investment objective, but unacceptable risk, given degree of cultural and organisational change required.
Preferred way forward	Option 1.4 is the preferred way forward
Next action: option 1.4 gets carried forward for analysis as preferred scope	Option 1.4 now provides the preferred scope within which to analyse potential technical options

In the case of IS, the degree of support required might extend from the delivery of IS (systems and support functions) to the delivery of service outputs (reports, etc.).

Case study

The Prison Service decided that their choice of services in relation to business needs should be assessed on a continuum. This included the options shown in Table 4.6.

Technical options

This set of options describes the **what** in terms of the **how**, i.e. potential technical solutions delivering the preferred scope. For example, in response to a particular service requirement – the need to store, retrieve and communicate information – the service solution to be adopted could be as shown in Table 4.7.

The extent to which the technical options need to be thought through in this way has been clouded rather by the arrival of the PFI as a method of service delivery within the public sector. The principle that the public sector procurer should focus on service outputs rather than service inputs, and rely on the private sector to innovate with respect to the technical solutions, has in some instances been misconstrued for a number of reasons.

Table 4.7: Solution delivering the means to store, retrieve and communicate information

Solution sets	Description
Paper-based solution	Manual files
CD ROMs	A relatively low cost and risk-free technical solution
Electronic file servers	Storage and communication of information within the organisation by means of a local area network (LAN)
Web browsers and Internet-based solution	The ability to be able to communicate information externally with customers and other stakeholders

First, the public sector still needs to be an intelligent customer, which means it must understand the potential solutions for meeting service needs. Second, the public sector organisation is still required to construct an in-house solution (the public sector comparator) to the output-based specification (OBS) for gauging value for money comparison. This should not emulate the service provider's solution. Finally, it should be remembered that the vast majority of public sector investments are still procured by conventional means.

The range of technical solution sets will vary depending on:

- the availability of new ways of working
- the availability of new technologies
- the extent to which the existing technical infrastructure, applications and other resources can be utilised.

Table 4.8: Potential technical solutions delivering the preferred scope

Starting point	*Description*
Business scope and key service requirements (option 1.4)	Provision of basic Electronic Prisoner Record plus: • coverage of all operational services • all prison locations • full range of service streams • all existing and new processes
Service solutions (2)	*Description*
Option 2.1	Use of existing IT systems plus minimum investment in new IS/IT system components.
Option 2.2	Use of existing IT systems plus intermediate investment in IS/IT on system components and new services (helpdesk and training)
Option 2.3	Replacement of existing systems in new system, plus full range of IS/IT services (helpdesk, training and future software development)
Preferred way forward Next action: options 1.4 and 2.2 get carried forward and provide the preferred way forward within which to analyse potential methods of service delivery	Option 2.2 was selected as the preferred option. It had the best balance of costs, benefits and risks. We have deliberately omitted the details of the decision-making process for purposes of brevity.

Research into available technologies and the service solutions of other organisations, particularly those in a similar sector, will inform and shape the investor's judgement. In addition, the use of market soundings of potential service providers and suppliers will help to inform the available technical solutions.

Case study

Taking forward their preferred scope (option 1.4), the prison service considered and appraised the technical solutions shown in Table 4.8.

Service delivery options

This set of options describes the possible options for service delivery, i.e. the **what** in terms of the **who**.

The days when in-house provision was the favoured solution are gone. Public and private sector organisations now routinely consider the merits of outsourcing and – to a lesser extent – strategic partnerships with other organisations. Within the public sector, there are now a number of public– private partnership (PPP) arrangements on offer, including PFI.

By way of illustration, a government department considering the replacement and upgrading of its existing IS/IT might consider the main options shown in Table 4.9.

The range of potential options to be considered for service delivery will vary depending on:

- the level of attendant risks and the potential for value for money through risk transfer
- the level of capabilities and competence within the organisation, in terms of the skills required to provide and manage the required services
- the degree to which the required services form part of the core business of the organisation and provide holistic fit.

Options for service delivery require some imagination and knowledge of what is happening within the marketplace. It will not be sufficient to replicate what others have achieved: the circumstances of all organisations vary.

From the standpoint of the public sector, it should be recognised that all political parties are in favour of PPPs, where it can be demonstrated that these arrangements make strategic sense, improve the quality of public services and offer the taxpayer improved value for money.

Table 4.9: Potential options for upgrading IS/IT

Potential options	Description
In-house provision	Hardware and software applications purchased from the capital budget and supported, operationally, in-house
Outsource/facilities management	Hardware and software applications purchased from the capital budget and supported externally by another organisation
IT partnership	IT provided by an external provider on a relatively short-term contract
IS/IT strategic partnership	IS provided by an external provider on a relatively long contract. IT an integral part of the service. Partner to have a voice in the strategic direction of the required services
Business partnership	One stage further. Elements of the business undertaken by the strategic partner on a long-term basis. IS/IT could be considered as one of the supporting components for service provision

Case study

Taking forward their preferred scope (option 1.4) and technical solution (option 2.2), the prison service decided that the potential options for service delivery were as shown in Table 4.10.

Implementation options

This set of options describes the time-scales within which the required services could be implemented in accordance with business constraints, i.e. 'the **what** in terms of the **when**'.

Options range from full implementation of the total package of services on the go-live date for the project to partial implementation of modules and/or increments of services within the package. Once the modules and/or increments have been developed, consideration should be given to piloting, phased roll-out and 'big-bang' implementation.

Table 4.10: Potential options for service delivery

Starting point	Description
Business scope and key service requirements (option 1.4)	Provision of basic Electronic Prisoner Record plus: • coverage of all operational services • all prison locations • full range of service streams • all existing and new processes
Technical solution (option 2.2)	• use of existing IT systems plus intermediate investment in new services

Service delivery options (3)	Description
Option 3.1	IS strategic partnership: long-term contract and operational responsibility for all IS/IT services, including specified business outputs
Option 3.2	IT partner or outsource: medium-term contract for IT services
Option 3.3	In-house provision: all business and IS/IT services to remain with the organisation
Preferred way forward Next action: options 1.4, 2.2 and 3.1 get carried forward to the next stage and provide the way forward for analysis of implementation options	Option 3.1 is the preferred way forward. It best meets the strategic needs of the prison service and provides the starting point for the transfer of other services following the successful completion of this project. Option 3.2 was considered to be too limited in scope and risky. Option 3.3 was judged to be unrealistic given the low level of available skills in-house

---

Box 4.4: Distinction between modular and incremental approaches

Modular approach

This is a discrete part of the project scope which is valuable in its own right even if the other parts of the project scope are not undertaken. For example, a degree course in economics at master's level typically includes microeconomics, macroeconomics, statistical methods/mathematical economics/econometrics, a dissertation and a couple of optional subjects (public sector economics, monetary economics, development economics, etc.). Completion of any of these modules offers some value but the full suite is required to meet the requirement of a master's degree. In principle, one could pursue individual modules until the full degree requirement is met (if only universities were this flexible). In IT projects, an example for an office information system is to offer a spreadsheet package (say EXCEL) in the first instance. Other modules, word-processing, etc., may be offered later.

Incremental approach
This would initially deliver a reduced scope for each module in the degree programme, thereby offering a subset of the benefits for the particular modules. Once this has been successfully delivered, the rest of the module could be delivered. In IT projects, this is equivalent to offering systems with basic functionalities in the first instance. Other, more advanced, functions could be added later once the risks become better understood.

Implementation options are particularly important, given the number of IT and other project failures which have made news headlines in recent years. The study undertaken by the government's CITU, *Successful IT: modernising government in action*, recommends 'Departments and agencies must adopt a modular and/or incremental approach to projects, unless there are very strong reasons for not doing so' (p. 36).

Implementation options will vary depending on:

- Business needs and affordability. Some operational needs require to be satisfied immediately, whereas others might be phased in over a period of time commensurate with service requirements and affordability constraints.
- The associated business risks, including the ability to cope with service change. The introduction of services must be aligned with the organisation's ability to cope with the pace of required change. Often, this change must be planned for as part of a business change management programme.
- Supply-side capability and capacity and associated service risks. The ability of service provider(s) to introduce the required degree of change. For example, the design and build of new services.

Organisations will find it useful to model different scenarios. The key to the preferred option is a delicate balance of risk and reward, commensurate with business needs for the planned services and VFM.

Case study

Taking forward their preferred scope (option 1.4), technical solution (option 2.2) and method of service delivery (option 3.1), the prison service considered the implementation options shown in Table 4.11.

Table 4.11: Potential options for implementation

Starting point	Description
Business scope and key service requirements (option 1.4)	Provision of basic Electronic Prisoner Record plus: <ul><li>coverage of all operational services</li><li>all prison locations</li><li>full range of service streams</li><li>all existing and new processes</li></ul>
Technical solution (option 2.2)	<ul><li>use of existing IT systems plus intermediate investment in new services</li></ul>
Service delivery (option 3.1)	<ul><li>IS strategic partnership</li></ul>

Implementation options (4)	Description
Option 4.1	Full implementation of the contracted service in year 1
Option 4.2	Phased implementation: <ul><li>core services within main prison – year 1</li><li>existing processes only – year 1</li><li>remaining services – year 2</li></ul>
Option 4.3	Phased implementation: <ul><li>core services within main prison – year 1</li><li>existing and new processes – year 1</li><li>remaining services – within 18 months of start</li></ul>
Preferred way forward Next action: options 1.4, 2.2, 3.1 and 4.2 are taken forward to the next stage and provide the preferred way forward within which to analyse funding options	The preferred option was option 4.3, since this met the investment objectives in full and provided the new services required within the specified time-scale without undue risks to the organisation and suppliers option 4.1 is considered too risky option 4.2 does not provide all the services required in sufficient time

Funding options

This set of options considers the available methods of funding, or financing, for the preferred way forward thus far. The aim is to select the best method of funding the project, recognising that this, too, is a value-for-money decision.

Numerous options exist for the funding of investments. For public sector projects, these include exchequer capital funds, donations/sponsorship funds, traditional lease, private finance under the aegis of PFI and 'hybrid funds' (i.e. combinations of conventional public finance and private finance).

The possibility of involving the private sector through strategic partnerships, facilities management and outsourcing should always be considered as part of the service delivery layer of the options framework. Similarly, private finance options should be considered as a matter of course in accordance with government policy.

If preliminary investigations indicate that there are good grounds for ruling out some or all of the potential private financing options on strategic or value-for-money grounds, it may be not be necessary to pursue them further. However, the possibility of reconsidering the involvement of the private sector in light of changing circumstances should be kept under review as the procurement unfolds. In all cases, the reasons for rejecting private finance should be fully recorded.

Case study

Taking forward their preferred scope (option 1.4), technical solution (option 2.2), method of service delivery (option 3.1) and implementation option (option 4.3), the prison service considered the funding options shown in Table 4.12.

Preferred way forward

The preferred way forward indicates our best assessment of the possible scope, technical solution, method of service delivery, implementation and funding, in terms of meeting the investment objectives, business priorities and CSFs for the proposed investment.

Using the options framework, we have arrived at this conclusion by selecting the choice which provides best fit in each tier of the model, and subjecting our choice to the next level of the model. The preferred way forward has thus emerged systematically and logically following a SWOT analysis of available options in each tier.

Table 4.12: Potential options for funding

Starting point	Description
Business scope and key service requirements (option 1.4)	Provision of basic Electronic Prisoner Record plus: ● coverage of all operational services ● all prison locations ● full range of service streams ● all existing and new processes
Technical solution (option 2.2)	● use of existing IT systems plus intermediate investment in new services
Service delivery (option 3.1)	● IS strategic partnership
Implementation (option 4.2)	● phased implementation
Funding options (5)	Description
Option 5.1	Public capital
Option 5.2	Private finance, PFI (PPP)
Preferred way forward for short-listing and preparation of appraisals	The preferred option is option 5.2, since the scope for significant service risk is likely to make this the most affordable and attractive option on VFM grounds. Option 5.1 was tested through the provision of a PSC

At this stage in the development of the case for change, we have now determined the most realistic, reliable and pragmatic way forward for meeting the business needs and service requirements of the organisation. This conclusion now needs to be tested with greater rigour.

Case study

The prison service decided that their preferred way forward should be documented within a SOC for the agreement and approval of their management board. They anticipated this would help to engender senior management commitment and buy-in to the proposed solution.

However, from the standpoint of the project team, the important point was that they now knew where they were going and how they would get there. This was as shown in Table 4.13.

Table 4.13: The preferred way forward

	Preferred way forward
Business scope and high-level service requirements	Provision of Basic Electronic Prisoner Record plus: • coverage of all operational services • all prison locations • full range of service streams • all existing and new processes
Technical solution	Use of existing IT systems plus intermediate investment in IS/IT on system components and new services (helpdesk and training)
Service delivery	An IS strategic partnership arrangement
Implementation	Phased implementation: • core services within main prison – year 1 • existing and new processes – year 1 • remaining services – within 18 months of start
Funding	The use of private finance

The team was now conscious of the need to test its preferred way forward for value-for-money and affordability purposes. It required, therefore, to be fully costed and subjected to accepted investment appraisal tools and techniques as part of the short list for the procurement.

Short-listed options

From the long list of options identified via the options framework or the conventional approach, the aim should now be to select a manageable short-list for more detailed assessment. We recommend four options, including the 'do nothing' or 'do minimum' for the short-list.

Based on the prison service case study, we have demonstrated how this can be done using the options framework. The Department of Health's Capital Investment Manual recommends an alternative approach. As already noted, this approach relies on a random process, which involves brain-storming to generate options. There is thus a risk of overlooking genuine options. Regardless of which approach is adopted, it is important to assess each option in terms of how well it meets the investment objectives, benefits criteria and other CSFs for the project.

Although the costs of options will not have been identified explicitly at this stage, it should be possible to sift the long list and eliminate options that are clearly unaffordable, fail to satisfy the principal investment objectives of the project, violate important constraints or which, when compared with another option, are clearly inferior. Inferiority can be demonstrated in two ways: either in terms of fewer benefits delivered at higher or equal cost, or an equivalent amount of benefits delivered at a higher cost. If options are similar, in that they provide comparable benefits by the same method, a single representative option should be identified and used in subsequent stages of analysis.

Options which are chosen at this stage, whether based on the options framework or a number of representative options as described in the conventional approach, will then undergo formal cost–benefit analysis (CBA). The reasons for discarding options should be explicitly recorded. The tools and techniques for undertaking a CBA are summarised in Chapter 8. Further details may be found in HM Treasury's 'Green Book' (1997).

Case study

In the case of the prison service, they selected five options for the short list. These were as follows:

1 the 'do nothing' or 'do minimum' – as a baseline for VFM
2 the preferred way forward or PSC – shown above, and two further options, both variants of the preferred way forward
3 the PSC – a *more ambitious* approach
4 the PSC – a *less ambitious* approach, and
5 the PSC (PFI) option that emerged from market soundings.

In the case of the more ambitious option, the full scope and range of services was selected (option 1.5 in the case study) for implementation in the shortest possible time-scale (option 4.1). For the less ambitious option, the minimum scope and level of services (option 1.3) was chosen for implementation in the shortest possible time-scale (option 4.2). The PSC (privately financed) option was calculated on the basis of PFI costs provided by service providers during market soundings. A PIN was used for this purpose.

The prison service summarised their economic appraisals over a ten-year time horizon as shown in Table 4.14.

The prison service provided a full description of costs and benefits, costing assumptions and the discount rate used.

In this instance, PFI costings for each option were unavailable so the PSCs were calculated solely on a publicly funded basis.

Table 4.14: Economic appraisals over a ten-year time horizon

Options	Option 1 (status quo)	Option 2 (PSC – expected)	Option 3 (PSC – less ambitious)	Option 4 (PSC – more ambitious)	Option 5 (Best PFI solution)
Costs					
Initial capital costs					
Opportunity cost					
Replacement costs					
Residual values					
Staff costs					
Operating costs					
Cost of risk retained					
Project management					
Evaluation					
Less benefits					
Cash-releasing					
Non-cash-releasing					
Net present value					

Coverage of costs and benefits

Capital cost

These included the following main items:

- **Initial capital costs:** IT development (staff and consultancy fees); purchases of hardware and software; installation; special furniture and work services.
- **Opportunity costs:** Economic costs (value in most valuable alternative use) based on up-to-date valuations of capital assets already in the prison's ownership – land, buildings and equipment.
- **Replacement costs:** These included the cost for replacement capital assets during the ten-year appraisal period.
- **Residual value:** Assets were depreciated annually in accordance with departmental policy and the residual value of assets shown at the close of the investment period.

Current costs

These included the following main items:

- **Staff costs:** Project management, other management and operational costs incurred over the ten-year period.
- **Operating costs:** Other recurring non-staff costs: training; maintenance charges; licensing and support costs; leasing and rental costs; rates; energy; cleaning for new IT accommodation.
- **Risk:** The cost of risk retained, which will vary from solution to solution depending on its scope, complexity and extent to which it will be shared with potential service providers.
- **Wider public sector costs:** Costs falling to other parts of the wider public sector and private sector.

Benefits

These included the following quantifiable (£) benefits:

- **Cash-releasing savings:** Reduction in the manpower complement of the prison service as a direct result of the improved use of IT.
- **Non-cash-releasing savings:** Number of posts in the prison service which could be switched to other operations, including the introduction of improved services as a result of the improved use of IT.
- **Wider public sector benefits:** Benefits accruing to other public sector organisations, private sector contractors and prisoner families.

Costing assumptions

Costs and benefits were valued on an economic cost or opportunity cost basis so that all the resources used and released by the options were considered.

Specific points included the following:

- **Prices:** Current market prices were used to reflect economic costs.

- **Public sector assets:** The valuations for the opportunity costs of assets already in public ownership were provided by the landlord and IT suppliers.
- **Sunk costs:** Costs already incurred on the staffing of the project to date were excluded.
- **Taxes and subsidies:** VAT, transfer payments (social security benefits) and redundancy payments were excluded.
- **Salary costs:** The economic cost was calculated using the departmental ready reckoner. This included National Insurance and employers' superannuation contributions and common overheads.
- **Consultants:** These were calculated at fee rate, including overheads
- **Inflation:** This was excluded, with the exception of rises above the retail price index for specific commodities.

Discount rate

The discount rate used was the standard 6% used within the public sector. This was verified with the department's economists in accordance with the Treasury's 'Green Book'.

Benefits appraisal

Benefits that can be quantified in the financial sense, e.g. cash-releasing and non-cash-releasing (£) benefits – both direct and indirect to the organisation – should be included in the economic appraisals and the cost–benefit analysis of options. However, in many investment proposals, some benefits are not amenable to monetary valuations. Notable examples include: the future proofing of the organisation; improvements in staff morale and customer relations; the ability to respond more effectively to unexpected business change; and improved accuracy of records.

   A method in common use within investment appraisal is to weight and score the non-quantifiable benefits for each option (*see* Chapter 8). This is preferable to ranking the benefits, because placing them in their order of priority, from greatest to least value, does not in itself provide any objective assessment of how they vary from option to option.

Case study

The prison service convened a workshop made up of key stakeholders. It was drawn from headquarters staff, governors, local staff and social services. Understandably, prisoners and their families were excluded, even though they were, arguably, an important group of stakeholders.

The following approach to the weighting and scoring of options is recommended and was adopted by the prison service:

- **Step 1:** The individual benefits for the weighting and scoring of options were brigaded by key stakeholder group (or beneficiary) and confirmed by the entire workshop.
- **Step 2:** The workshop divided into different groups – business, user and technical. Each group gave a weight (%) to each benefit criterion on a scale of 0 to 100.
- **Step 3:** Each group then assigned a raw score (1 to 10) against each benefit criteria.
- **Step 4:** The weights and scores were then multiplied to provide a total weighted score for each option.
- **Step 5:** The options were then ranked in terms of total scores against the agreed benefit criteria and the preferred option – that with the highest total weighted score – was selected.
- **Step 6:** Key difference among the groups were discussed and resolved. The results were recorded, including any items which could not be resolved.

Risk assessment

The service risks (design, build, financial and operational) associated with each option need to be evaluated, since the key risks – the 20% which account for 80% of the risk values – will vary in terms of their value (£), potential impact and the extent to which they can be shared with potential service providers.

In the past, the most widely used technique for assessing risk and uncertainty has been sensitivity analysis. However, it is now accepted that the cost of risks retained under each option should be accounted for within the economic appraisals. This helps to establish the true cost of a project, regardless of whether it is privately or publicly funded. It also helps to evaluate value for money when publicly funded options are compared with privately financed options. Prior to the advent of PFI, in the vast majority of cases, no allowance was made for the cost of risk retained by the public sector. Yet we now know that the cost of risk retained by the public sector

Table 4.15: The main risks associated with the PSC

High-level risk category	Description of key risks	Value £
1 Design risks	• Systems not designed to specification	
2 Construction and development risk	• Late delivery of systems and associated services	
	• Higher-than-expected construction costs	
3 Transition and implementation risk	• Training not delivered to time-scale, etc.	
	• Rejection of systems by employees	
4 Availability and performance risk	• Performance rates unacceptable	
	• Availability rates unacceptable	
	• Failure to deliver agreed changes during the contract period	
5 Operating risks	• Loss of key staff and skill shortages	
	• Higher-than-expected operating costs, including agreed change	
	• Security and privacy issues	
	• System maintenance unacceptable	
6 Variability of revenue risk	• Changes in expected use and volumes	
	• Changes in the expected number of sites	
	• Changes in the estimated revenues for new business and third-party revenue streams	
	• Unexpected changes in the range required	
7 Termination risks	• Termination due to default by organisation	
	• Termination due to default by supply side	
8 Technology obsolescence risks	• Failure of systems to deliver agreed outputs	
9 Control risks	• Failure to control or manage services provided for in the output-based specifications	
10 Residual value risks	• Non-requirement for the use of the assets at the end of the contracted period	
11 Financing risks	• Non-availability of the required capital	
12 Legislative risks	• Changes in primary legislation leading to cost increases	
	• Changes in primary legislation leading to cost increases	
13 Other project risks	• Poor project management	
	• Non-realisation of benefits – quantifiable benefits (direct and indirect)	
	• Non-realisation of benefits – qualitative benefits (direct and indirect)	

on public sector procurements is conservatively estimated at between 15 and 40% of anticipated costs.

Tools and techniques for identifying, quantifying and apportioning risks to the party best placed to manage the risk are provided in Chapter 8. However, in the case of risks that cannot be quantified, it may be necessary to weight and score the risks in a manner somewhat similar to that for non-financial benefits.

Case study

Using the 13 key categories of risk recommended for examination by the Treasury Select Committee for PFI (PPP) deals, the prison service listed the main risks associated with the PSC as shown in Table 4.15. These risks were drawn from an earlier examination of some 62 service risks in the design, build, finance and operational phases of the project.

The prison service augmented their risk analysis with a sensitivity analysis. The latter was performed on the risks that have been assessed to have relatively large values and those with uncertain probabilities and/or financial impacts. They also calculated the switching values or cross-over points. This showed the amount(s) by which the variable(s) under investigation would have to change in order to affect the ranking of the options.

The preferred option

If the required analyses have been rigorously undertaken, selecting the preferred option should be a relatively straightforward step in the decision-making process, on the basis of the results of the discounted cash-flows, analysis of non-financial benefits, risk analysis and sensitivity analysis for each option.

The final choice of the preferred option lies with senior management and possibly stakeholders, drawing on advice from their advisers. The business case should present the information succinctly and clearly to help managers reach a decision about the preferred option.

The normal decision-making rule is to select the option which yields the highest positive net present value (NPV). This option affords the greatest ratio of benefits over costs. Alternatively, if all the short-listed options deliver the same quantum of benefits but at differential costs (including risks), then the decision rule is to select the option with the lowest net present cost. It is important to ensure that this option is also affordable. Affordability issues are addressed in Chapter 6.

Table 4.16:

Evaluation results	Option 1 (status quo)	Option 2 (PSC)	Option 3 (PSC – less ambitious)	Option 4 (PSC – more ambitious)	Option 5 (PSC – privately financed)
Benefits evaluation					
Economic appraisals					
Ratio of benefits to costs					
Ranking					
Risk evaluation					
Sensitivity analysis					
Overall ranking					

Case study

Using Table 4.16, the prison service ranked the options in order of their attendant costs, benefits and risks.

Conclusion

The key points from this chapter may be summarised as follows.

- The economic case must be based on sound investment appraisal principles. The conventions laid down in HM Treasury's 'Green Book' should be followed closely.
- It is important to define comprehensive and meaningful benefit criteria and critical success factors to facilitate assessment of the options. *The wrong CSFs will inevitably lead to the wrong choice.*
- Ensure that the widest range of possible options is identified and appraised at the outset. The options framework provides an approach to ensuring important options are not overlooked.
- Investment objectives must not be so narrowly defined as to rule out important options; on the other hand, objectives which are too broad create unnecessary work and lose credibility.
- Think in terms of how best to maximise benefits, both quantifiable and qualitative, throughout the process. This applies to the long list as well as the short-listed options.

- Equally, the risks associated with any proposed way forward should be considered throughout. The key to success is not the best storyline, but a project that can be delivered successfully once it has been approved and proceeds to the implementation stage.
- It is good practice to prepare a public sector comparator, or its equivalent, to serve as a benchmark for gauging value for money. Ensure the PSC does not mimic solutions offered by bidders during the tendering process and include a privately financed option, if possible.
- Present the results of the economic appraisal clearly. The reasons for selection of the preferred option must be explicitly recorded. The same applies to options which have been sifted out.
- Avoid choosing the preferred option on the basis of preconceptions. Preconceived solutions are easily spotted by skilled reviewers at the approval stage, and will lead to prolonged delays in securing approval to proceed to the implementation phase.

CHAPTER FIVE

The commercial case

The key to a successful project is the deal itself, which is normally reflected in a commercial contract. This chapter provides guidance on how the deal should be approached. In the past, partly on account of lack of relevant skills, contractual issues have not been approached with rigour or an appreciation of commercial realities. Consequently, projects have often been brilliantly scoped and planned in many cases, but failed to realise their potential or see the light of day. This chapter provides a number of tips to bring about win–win outcomes for the procuring organisation and suppliers.

Introduction

Governments are increasingly becoming reliant on the private sector to satisfy their business needs. In the UK, for example, this is certainly the case with information technology projects. The success of the PFI and, more generally, public–private partnerships has accelerated this trend.

The importance of developing effective relationships with suppliers and negotiating sound deals cannot be overstated. By a 'sound deal', we mean much more than the financial aspects of the deal. This must necessarily encompass the way the deal is scoped, the capability of suppliers, the quality of the solutions on offer, their understanding of the procuring organisation's business needs, their ability to work effectively with the procuring organisation as a 'marriage partner' and integrate their solution with the client's business processes, and the way the whole procurement process is managed.

The aim of the commercial case is to secure the optimal deal for both the procuring organisation and the selected service provider. Failure to secure a 'win–win' outcome and to develop 'shared goals' will make for an uneasy partnership arrangement as the 'loser' will not have an incentive to make the deal work in practice. The key issues which should be addressed as part of the commercial case are summarised in Box 5.1. We will discuss each issue in turn and provide guidance and tips for delivering the desired required outcomes.

Box 5.1: Scope of the commercial case

- Scope and services
- Charging mechanisms
- Risk transfer
- Key contractual arrangements
- Personnel implications
- Implementation time-scales
- Accountancy treatment

Scope and services

The purpose of this section is to capture the scope and content of the desired deal. Regardless of the method of procurement adopted, there are a number of fundamental principles to bear in mind:

- Requirements must be specified as far as possible in terms of the desired outcomes and outputs to be produced. The focus should not be on the processes which produce them or the technology required.
- The quality attributes of the services required and the performance measures against which they will be assessed must be specified.
- The deal must allow scope for the prospective service providers to suggest innovative ways of meeting the service requirements, including proposals which require rethinking of the business processes within the customer organisation.

This section of the business case must briefly summarise:

- the business area affected by procurement
- the business environment and related activites
- the business objectives relevant to the procurement affected by the procurement
- scope of the procurement
- specification of outputs
- requirements to be met – essential outputs, performance measures, quality attributes
- stakeholders for the outputs
- possibilities: options for variation in the scope of the procurement
- future developments required

- requirements/constraints for migration, implementation, start-up, etc.
- requirements for additional services
- scope for the transfer of assets and other resources, etc.
- risk transfer arrangements.

Payment mechanisms

This section should record the relevant charging or payment mechanisms. This boils down to a statement of the client's preferred way to pay for the deal and required services.

The payment mechanism is the formula against which payment for the contracted services will be made. The underlying aim of the payment mechanism and pricing structure is to underpin the optimum balance between risk and return in the contract. As a general principle, the approach should be to relate payment to the delivery of service outputs and performance of the service provider.

What we pay and how we pay for an agreed level of service is an integral part of VFM. If properly constructed, the payment mechanism will incentivise the service provider to deliver services in accordance with the business imperatives of the organisation

In deals progressed thus far, a number of key elements stand out in the underlying payment mechanism. These elements focus on different phases of the project:

- The pre-delivery phase – up to acceptable delivery of the service and commencement of the payment stream.
- The operational phase – following acceptable delivery of the service up until the close of the primary contractual period.
- The extension phase – post primary contractual period.

The pre-delivery phase

Fixed price/costs

The service provider must be provided with the incentive to deliver services to time and cost. Deals will, therefore, involve a fixed price and fixed timetable for the delivery of agreed outputs, with appropriate remedies in place for delays and cost over-runs.

Payment on delivery of outputs

Payment will be linked to the delivery of service outputs and will not commence until the contracted service comes on stream. In the case of many hospital deals, where a suite of services is being procured, payment may be staggered against the delivery of key outputs within the overall implementation programme for the complete service. However, the guiding principle remains that a revenue stream to the service provider should only commence when a benefit stream commences on the part of the public sector organisation. A service that fails to perform could result in termination of all the payment streams and rights to the assets in extreme cases.

The operational phase

Availability payment

This element links service delivery to the agreed availability criteria. For example, in the case of a hospital information support system (HISS), the client could stipulate that the service must be available a minimum of 95% of the time between contracted hours. The procuring organisation will need to negotiate service-level agreements which outline availability criteria, and in some cases it may be appropriate to treat availability as a threshold which releases a payment stream based on other factors, for example, performance or throughput. Failure on the part of the service provider to meet availability criteria should lead to reduced payments and ultimately cessation of the service.

Performance payment

Performance payments, based on the service being able to meet specified performance targets, help to ensure that the service continues to deliver service outputs. These may be expressed, for example, in terms of system response times or each hospital transaction processed.

Transaction/volume payment

This element relates payment to the achievement of business benefit or to another identifiable measure of business outputs, for example, the number of transactions processed. In most deals, it will be preferable to link payment to the productivity or usage of the service. Linking payment to productivity provides the service provider with the incentive to optimise the level of productivity and also to invest further if increased levels of productivity are required.

Incentive payment

Significant benefits can also accrue from making as much payment as possible dependent on the overall performance of the organisation's business processes. This may involve the organisation and service provider sharing in the level of benefits that accrue.

Cost of change

The cost of change has been a major risk for public sector organisations in the past. Mechanisms may be developed that minimise the effects of business change on the cost of the service. For example, the benchmarking and market testing on a regular basis. Service providers may be provided with the incentive to build flexible services and systems which are receptive to change.

Third-party revenues

Mechanisms can also be constructed in the contract to provide the service provider with the incentive to develop and exploit alternative revenue streams and new business. For example, providers might be permitted to sell data in an aggregated form, to market the software solution elsewhere or to utilise service capacity elsewhere. By giving the provider the freedom to exploit such opportunities, the price for the core service will reduce and the value for money improve.

The extension phase

Technological obsolescence

In the operational phase, the service provider is delivering the service for an agreed payment stream. If investment in new technology will reduce fixed costs then the service provider's profit margin will increase. This provides a natural incentive to invest in new technology.

Moreover, if the payment mechanism is related to the effective usage of the system, then investment in technology over the contract period could improve the scope for productivity. This, in turn, would increase the service provider's return and increase benefit to the public sector.

Two other contractual devices can help to encourage the service provider to consistently upgrade the service:

- First, various upgrades could be included within the initial price to ensure the service is kept up to date.
- Second, an element of the service provider's initial recoverable investment, i.e. the return required from providing the service, could be deferred to the end of the contractual period.

The amount of this payment – the transfer payment – could be bid competitively during the first competition and put at risk during subsequent recompetitions. The risk of losing the transfer payment provides the service provider with the incentive to upgrade the service so that it is competitive at the close of the initial contract period. In reality, though, this mechanism has been difficult to implement sensibly in practice.

Contract currencies

Contract currencies are variable measures which underpin the payment mechanism and the transfer of risk by making them meaningful and effective in the service contract.

The aim should be to choose contract currencies which demonstrate productivity and performance. Productivity can be measured through input: output, where the measures of both are constant over the implementation and ongoing performance of the service. This means that measures – or contract currencies – must be those elements where improvement is desired. All measures must be backed up by minimum service levels to guarantee the desired levels of performance, availability and accuracy from the service. The key is, therefore, to choose comparative measures which provide service providers with the incentive to improve. In other words, a reduced payment for underperformance and increased payment for performance in excess of the minimum required.

Input measures relate to the response time of services, for example applications important to the business process and the time spent in applications to produce outputs.

Examples of constituent factors in developing these measures for IM&T deals are as follows:

- megabytes used in specific applications
- length of time logged on to specific applications
- average load during office hours on the Local Area Network
- response times to entry of application
- time spent on applications to produce specified outputs
- transactions achieving target response times
- number of transactions handled per day.

All these measures begin on the invocation of certain applications. The aim for the service provider should be to reduce time in applications for the same or increased output, since this leads to improved payment. Conversely, any down time would lose the service provider input time and ultimately result in reduced payment.

In contrast to 'input measures', the key to output currencies is that they are identifiable outputs from a business process. If output improves while input stays constant, productivity should improve.

Examples of possible output measures for a Hospital Information Support System include:

- number of documents (medical records) produced
- number of forms (medical entries) processed in data entry
- documents (patient records) stored on file (either electronic storage or paper copy for file)
- number of documents 'saved' or stored on the system
- amount or volume of user data stored
- number of pages printed
- number of management reports run
- pages of report run
- size of file-able transactions
- entries to final application (e.g. patient record).

These are only shown by way of illustration. The aim should be to continuously improve, rather than replicate, these measures.

Overarching input: output currencies might be usability measures such as:

- proportion of users (nursing and administrative staff) requiring assistance
- proportion of new users (doctors, nurses, and administrative personnel) able to use the system without assistance following agreed training.
- number of complaints from doctors, nurses and administrative personnel to the help desk
- proportion of users expressing satisfaction within user surveys etc.

Risk transfer

This section of the business case is an extension of the risk sections of the strategic and economic cases. Within the strategic case, the focus is on high-level identification and assessment of strategic and business-related risks. Within the economic case, the emphasis is on more detailed risk identification and evaluation, not just 'strategic risks'. Within the commercial case, the main focus is on risk sharing.

In early versions of the business case, this will show how service (design, build, financial and operational) risks might be shared with the service provider. In subsequent versions, more detail will emerge, eventually leading to a matrix showing how risks have been apportioned in the agreed deal.

In practice, it should be noted that many of the risks associated with the provisions of services will be shared between both parties. The principle remains, however, that the aim should be to transfer risk to the party best able to manage the risk.

Key contractual arrangements

The key contractual arrangements should be summarised in the business case and should comply with the standard terms developed by the Treasury Task Force. These will, of course, differ from project to project; but in most instances the principal areas of the contract can be categorised as follows:

- duration of contract
- the provider's responsibilities in the delivery of the agreed services
- the payment mechanism
- the organisation's remedies in the event of failure by the provider to perform the services
- the relationship between the two parties in respect of any intellectual property rights
- compliance with any appropriate regulations
- the operational and contract administration elements of the terms and conditions
- the resolution of disagreements between the parties
- a matrix showing the agreed risk allocation
- options at the end of the contract.

The contract will generally be split into the main contract and various schedules. The main body of the contract will take precedence over the schedules in the event of any conflict between the parties. The key to successful completion of this section is simply to record the salient features of this documentation.

Personnel implications

Organisations may be legally and morally obliged to involve their staff and their representatives in a process of continuous dialogue during a major procurement. This is particularly the case in respect of PFI (PPP) procurements.

Consequently, this section of the business case must make clear:

- whether Transfer of Undertakings (Protection of Employment) Regulations 1981 (TUPE) will apply, directly or indirectly, to any staff transferring to the private sector as a result of the project, and that all the necessary regulations have been taken fully into account
- details of any terms regarding subsequent transfers at market testing interval (if these apply)
- descriptions of terms regarding trade union recognition (if these apply)
- descriptions regarding requirements for broadly comparable pensions for staff upon transfer
- within the public sector, that Codes of Practice are in place for the well-being and management of staff. The case should confirm that these have been adhered to.

Implementation time-scales

This section should outline the key milestones for delivery of the project and related services. The focus here, however, is on the deal, not the detail of the accompanying project plans, which form part of the project management case.

Accountancy treatment

Assessment of the accounting treatment of a proposed deal is a vital guide to assessing the level of risk transferred and hence value for money in a procurement. This is particularly true in the case of PFI (PPP) procurements where the governing principle is that a successful PFI (PPP) project must be

Table 5.1: How to account for PFI transactions

Check-points	Procuring department/organisation	Auditor
Pre-Invitation to Negotiate (ITN)	Provide 'initial view' on likely accounting treatment based on draft ITN and Outline Business Case material. By this stage, there should be an indicative risk allocation matrix and a preliminary view of the expected structure of the contract	To provide comments on the validity of the procurer's initial assessment
Pre-best and final offer (BAFO)	Update preliminary view if terms of the Invitation to Tender (ITT) are significantly different from the ITN	To comment on procurer's initial view in light of the ITT
Post-BAFO	Update initial assessment to provide a 'provisional judgement' based on the design solution and the preferred bidder's financial models	To comment on whether the procurer's 'provisional judgement' is reasonable
Pre-contract signature	Provide a 'final judgement' based on the distribution of risks and rewards, and other material aspects of the contract	To comment on whether the procurer's final judgement is reasonable, subject to any late changes in the contract

for the provision of a service over a number of years rather than the purchase of an asset. A PFI (PPP) procurement which is simply for the purchase of an asset by the public sector under a financing arrangement is unlikely to offer optimum VFM.

Public sector organisations will undoubtedly require specialist advice and guidance in this area. This is available from HM Treasury and the OGC.

Procurers and their advisers are strongly advised to keep the auditors informed of the likely accounting treatment of the deal as the negotiations develop. The Treasury Task Force guidance on *How to Account for PFI Transactions* recommends at least four checkpoints (*see* Table 5.1).

Key summary points

The main points from this chapter may be summarised as follows:

- The deal must be commercially viable and should comply with the Treasury Task Force's standard contract terms.
- The deal must be considered at the earliest possible stage and the rudiments of the intended arrangement documented as part of the SOC. Relying on the service provider for innovation does not mitigate the organisation's need to be an intelligent customer.
- The procuring organisation must specify the desired business outcomes and service outputs required – the 'what' rather than the 'how'.
- Suitable payment mechanisms which incentivise the service provider and at the same time maximise VFM for the client should be adopted. Avoid reliance on legal redress.
- Ensure that the appropriate arrangements for staff affected by the procurement are considered and put in place from the outset.
- Professional advice should be sought in negotiating the deal and assessing its impact on the organisation's balance sheet.

CHAPTER SIX

The financial case

This chapter reinforces the importance of the affordability test and outlines the core requirements. It is futile to negotiate a sound VFM deal which meets the organisation's business requirements if it is not affordable. Conversely, an affordable deal which fails the VFM test will not impress HM Treasury and external auditors. Having developed the economic case and refined it in light of the commercial case, it is important to demonstrate that the preferred option is affordable. This is the main focus of the 'financial case'. It is important to stress at the outset that this part of the business case requires specialist input from accountants and financial specialists. The guidance in this chapter is not intended to be definitive. Our main aim is to heighten awareness of affordability issues in investment planning.

Introduction

The main purpose of this section of the business case is to demonstrate that the proposed investment is affordable. In the process, it assesses the impact of the proposed investment on the prices, income and expenditure account, and balance sheet of the organisation.

Affordability is a key constraint throughout the scoping of the project and should be documented at key stages within the business planning and procurement phases. Too often in the past, the perfect case for expenditure has been submitted for approval, only to be rejected on grounds of affordability gaps.

Focus of financial case

Many practitioners of investment appraisals often confuse the 'financial case' with the 'economic case'. A distinction between the two cases is in order.

Table 6.1: Comparison of the financial and economic cases

Financial case	Economic case
Focus	Focus
• Affordability and both resource and non-resource costs	• VFM and net present value (NPV) cash flows
Coverage	Coverage
• for the Organisation only, e.g. NHS trust (narrow coverage)	• for the national economy as a whole, e.g. NHS and health sector (wide coverage)
Relevant standards (for public sector)	Relevant standards (for public sector)
• HM Treasury Accounting Rules	• HM Treasury Green Book (*Appraisal and Evaluation in Central Government*)
Analysis: financial appraisals *Includes*:	Analysis: economic appraisals *Includes*:
• cash-releasing benefits • all costs (including transfer payments, e.g. VAT)	• all quantifiable costs, benefits and risks • excludes transfer payments (e.g. VAT)
Perspective	Perspective
• Microeconomic	• Macroeconomic

The economic case focuses on VFM, taking into account resource costs and benefits. In contrast, the financial case focuses on 'affordability' of the options appraised in the economic appraisal, particularly the preferred option. The costs and benefits appraised within the financial case reflect an accountancy-based perspective. Consequently, both resource and non-resource costs and benefits are factored into the analysis. For example, whereas we would exclude VAT and capital charges (including allowance for depreciation) from the economic appraisals, these costs must be included in the financial analysis, as they have a direct bearing on the affordability of the options under consideration.

Table 6.1 summarises some of the other key differences between the financial and economic cases.

Overview

This section of the business case is made up of the following key headings. Each is briefly explained, together with a brief description of the process for delivery of the required outcomes:

- financial modelling
- capital requirements
- net effect on prices
- impact on balance sheet
- impact on income and expenditure account
- overall affordability

Financial modelling

Before this section of the case can be completed, a financial model of the proposed investment needs to be built to provide a financial representation of the project. In its early stages, this comprises of a best guestimate of the likely impact and outcomes(s) of the proposed investment. This model should be revised as new and better information becomes available.

Specialist advice should be sought from accountants and financial advisers. We would expect the organisation's director of finance to play a lead role in building and maintaining the model. If external management consultants are appointed to undertake this work, the structure and inputs of the model should still be vetted by the Senior Responsible Officer (SRO) and the organisation's director of finance.

The minimum requirements for most projects are shown in Box 6.1.

Box 6.1: Minimum requirements for financial model

- recording a description of the model and the associated methodology
- agreeing and recording the underlying assumptions (interest rates, inflation, taxation, etc.)
- detailing the proposed funding structure
- preparing the input schedules (costs, benefits and a suitable allowance for risk)
- preparing the projected profit and loss account
- preparing balance sheet projections
- making cash-flow projections
- preparing funding schedules
- calculating project returns for the different elements of financing
- supporting schedules (e.g. loans, fixed assets, taxation, payment mechanism)

Capital and revenue requirements

Having calculated the cash flows for each option, including capital charges, VAT (recoverable and non-recoverable) and other non-resource costs and benefits, the organisation is now in a position to determine whether or not the best VFM option is affordable.

The investment will generally result in an increase in depreciation charges. Within many organisations, e.g. the NHS, there is also a requirement to realise a 6% return on the new assets. Key questions to consider are:

- How much capital resources are required to implement the preferred option?
- How does this compare with the capital ceiling which was originally specified for the project?
- If there is a capital shortfall, how will it be met?

This is not the end of the investigation. The revenue requirements of the project also need to be considered. Indeed, unlike the capital funds, which are one-off expenditures, revenue requirements will have to be afforded year on year throughout the full life of the project. The key issue is whether the organisation will have both the initial capital and sufficient income to meet the ongoing costs of the project.

Net effect on prices

To address the issue of affordability, an assessment should also be made of the net effect of the investment on prices to 'purchasers' of the organisation's services. Will the net revenue consequences increase, decrease or remain neutral? In general, public sector investments are difficult to justify if they lead to an increase in prices for the organisation's services.

Affordability problems are common in most public sector departments. It is one of the main reasons for delay at the point at which the business case is submitted for approval. Partly for this reason, HM Treasury and other approval bodies now expect business-case sponsors to obtain suitable letters of support from the main purchasers of the organisation's services. The letter should explicitly address whether they are willing and able to meet the revenue consequences of the project year on year. See Box 6.2 for issues to cover in a letter of commissioner support. There should also be evidence of collaborative planning in developing the business strategy and the particular investment in question.

Box 6.2: Issues to cover in a letter of commissioner support

A commissioner support letter should:

- demonstrate that the main commissioner and other commissioners in the local health economy have been actively involved in developing the scheme throughout its various stages
- confirm acceptance of the strategic objectives of the scheme, its functional content, size and underlying model of care
- confirm that the costs of the scheme can be contained within the available budget and the willingness and ability to pay for the services at the specified price level
- state the margins of leeway beyond which support must be re-validated
- demonstrate that suitable contingency arrangements are in place to work with the provider to address any current or unforeseen affordability pressures
- be provided by the appropriate individual(s) within the organisation (usually the Chief Executive Officer)

Managing affordability gaps

Affordability problems are most likely to occur in the early years of the project, i.e. the construction and development phase. Benefits are unlikely to be realised in large measure during this phase to offset the costs of the investment. During the operational phase, however, benefits can be expected to build up gradually reaching the point where the net impact on operating costs and prices to purchasers is negative. The typical pattern for IM&T investments is illustrated in Table 6.2.

If the affordability analysis reveals the preferred VFM option is not affordable, there are a number of potential remedies on offer. Options to consider include one or more of the following:

- Phase the preferred option differently.
- Adopt a different design solution.
- Alter the scope of the preferred option (e.g. alter the functional content or the quality or quantity of the services offered).
- Find additional sources of funds (e.g. disposal of surplus assets if available, revenue support from commissioners of the organisation's services).

- Consider a different way of funding the project (e.g. funding the project under the PFI avoids the need for substantial capital expenditure in the early years, and leads to a smoother and more predictable pattern of expenditure year on year).
- Negotiate more competitive or flexible prices from the service provider(s).
- Find other ways of reducing costs and/or increase cash-releasing savings.

The following points are worth noting from Table 6.2:

- Savings are shown as 'negative quantities'.
- There is a net increase in both revenue and capital costs in years 0, 1 and 2. Thereafter, the project produces a net saving in each of the remaining seven years.
- The increase in savings more than offset the net increase in costs in the first three years.

To manage the affordability problem in years 0, 1 and 2, the organisation in question has agreed to fund the additional costs from its cash-releasing savings programme (CRES). The organisation has an excellent record in achieving its CRES targets and has achieved over the past three financial years savings in the order of £1.5m per year. This is more than enough to offset the deficit.

For the sake of brevity, Table 6.2 does not show the capital and revenue implications of the other short-listed options. Neither does it provide the breakdown of the costs and benefits, nor their underlying assumptions and the conclusions from relevant sensitivity analysis. **Organisations are strongly recommended to provide this information**. This is important for a number of reasons:

- It provides vital comparative information about the merits and demerits of all short-listed options.
- It provides a clear audit trail for helping others to understand the rationale for the choice of the preferred option.
- It allows reviewers of the business case to assess the validity of the figures and to challenge them if need be.
- It reduces delays in the approval process.

Note, it is also important to record how the project will be funded. The implicit assumption in Table 6.2 is that the project will be publicly funded, hence the reason for capital expenditure in the first two years. If it were to be privately financed, all the costs would be 'revenue costs'. The investor's capital expenditure would be included in the 'unitary service charge'.

Table 6.2:   Affordability assessment for preferred option (based on IM&T case study)

Revenue costs summary £000	Year 0	Year 1	Year 2	Year 3	Year 4	Year 5	Year 6	Year 7	Year 8	Year 9
● Costs*	200	450	650	480	400	450	550	400	900	650
● IM&T savings**	nil	nil	−390	−500	−590	−400	−480	−480	−850	−570
● Other cash-releasing savings	nil	−50	−200	−150	−250	−340	−400	−390	−770	−430
Net additional revenue costs (£000)	200	400	60	−170	−440	−290	−330	−470	−720	−350
Capital costs summary £000										
● Hardware	100	100	35							
● Non-recoverable VAT	18	18	6							
Total capital costs £000	118	118	41							
Total capital and revenue costs £000	318	518	101	−170	−440	−290	−330	−470	−720	−496

*These include all revenue costs – software, consumables, data conversion, interfacing, consultancy, implementation support, training, project management, maintenance, capital charges (both interest and depreciation), etc.
**These include savings on current IM&T costs, savings on capital charges and recoverable VAT.

Organisations should not shy away from recording 'quality gains' to support the case for the preferred investment option. These benefits are just as important as cash-releasing benefits. As stated previously, many of the benefits from IM&T investments beyond the 'business process redesign' stage are strategic and not amenable to quantification. They mainly produce cultural changes and continuous 'quality improvements' across the organisation or groups of organisations as a whole

Impact on balance sheet and income and expenditure account

The impact of the project on the organisation's balance sheet and its income and expenditure account should also be assessed. The results should be summarised in the business case. It is important for this task to be performed by a qualified accountant who understands the project and the organisation's business.

Returning to the example shown in Table 6.2, we would expect this investment to increase the organisation's net assets in the first three years. Due to depreciation, this value will decrease year on year.

As noted in Chapter 5, where significant assets are an integral part of the service, their accounting treatment will need to be examined. This will require an independent opinion from the organisation's auditors.

Judging affordability

Assessing affordability requires sound judgement of the organisation's business and requires that:

- **The balance sheet has been organised correctly** and properly accounts for current assets, fixed assets, current liabilities, long-term liabilities and capital.
- **The balance sheet of the organisation is in a healthy state.**

This involves an assessment of working capital, which is defined as follows:

Working capital = Current assets − Current liabilities

An organisation should never run short of working capital or overcapitalise. This is a common reason for business failure. A ratio of current assets to current liabilities of 2:1 is generally agreed to be the minimum working capital ratio. The ratio is calculated as follows:

$$Working\ capital\ ratio = \frac{Current\ assets}{Current\ liabilities}$$

In fact, the working capital figure is considered so important that many organisations in the private sector (limited companies in particular) publish their balance sheets with current liabilities taken over and deducted from the asset side, which provides another ratio — the liquid capital ratio or acid test ratio:

$$Liquid\ capital\ ratio = \frac{Current\ assets - Stock}{Current\ liabilities}$$

- **The organisation is solvent** and can meet its debt obligation.

This means that the organisation can meet any debt obligations in the immediate future without jeopardising the liquidity of the business.

- **The organisation is not overtrading.**

This links in with over-capitalisation, where the organisation is running short of working capital as a result of having acquired too many assets, leaving itself short of cash for operational expenses.

In this situation, attention must be paid to the organisation's cash flow, but it is first necessary to consider the return on capital employed and the return on capital invested.

The return on capital employed enables us to compare the receipts (or profits) earned with the capital employed to earn them, and may be calculated as follows:

$$Return\ on\ capital\ employed = \frac{Net\ receipts\ (or\ profit)}{Capital\ employed}$$

The return on capital invested calculates what the return was overall on the capital used and takes into account the lost opportunity or 'opportunity cost' of the capital employed. As such it is calculated as follows:

$$Return\ on\ capital\ invested = \frac{(Net\ profit - Opportunity\ cost)}{Capital\ invested\ initially}$$

- **The cash flow of the organisation is sound.**

Assessing cash flow should take into account:

- the pattern of business activities and trading generally
- budgeting for cash flow: a forecast which looks ahead and envisages the likely income and expenditure
- assessment of the cash balance at the end of any particular period in time.

During the implementation phase of the project, the organisation might need to undertake some:

- cash-flow smoothing (purchasing and paying invoices during the good times and arranging for payments during the bad times)
- variance analysis (the comparison of actual outcomes to forecast outcomes, making adjustments to the situation overall as required). For example, this may require passing on increased costs to the customer, or alternatively reducing costs through improved business processes.

- **Allowance has been made for risks.**

There are a number of risks which could affect the affordability of the project. The business case should summarise the results of the risk and sensitivity analyses which underpin the financial case.

The risks will vary from project to project. For a capital project in the NHS, some key questions to consider in this regard are:

- Would the project be still affordable if capital costs were to be 10% higher than expected?
- What if expected savings were to fall by more than 5%?
- What circumstances might cause savings targets to be breached?
- What if income to the trust were to be reduced by 5% or more, e.g. due to changes in the main health authority's commissioning decisions?
- How likely are these outcomes? What if interest rates were to increase by 1%?
- Is there a robust strategy in place to guard against the above outcomes?

Conclusion

The key points from this chapter may be summarised as follows:

- Undertaking some form of financial modelling is vital to successful delivery of the project. The Millennium Dome project has fallen into disrepute as a consequence of poor financial modelling.
- Appreciate the fundamental difference between the economic appraisals (which assess VFM) and the financial appraisals (which assess affordability).
- Consider carefully where the funds to cover the proposed investment are to come from: a new investor, existing reserves or future receipts.
- Affordability is much more than simply a consideration of whether funds are available. An assessment of the impact on the balance sheet and income and expenditure account of the organisation needs to be undertaken.
- Calculate the appropriate accounting ratios to enable decision makers to assess robustness of the cash-flow forecasts.
- Develop solutions for managing affordability gaps.
- Make the best available use of internal financial expertise, seek external support where this is not available and obtain an opinion from your auditors before seeking approval.
- Obtain suitable letters of support from commissioners of your services before submitting the business case for approval.

CHAPTER SEVEN

The project management case

The project management case is concerned with achievability and successful delivery of the project. This is often considered as an after-thought, if at all. The high rate of project failure in both the public and private sectors is, therefore, no surprise. This chapter provides guidance on the requirements for an effective project management case.

Introduction

Project failures are all too common – some make the headlines, but the vast majority are quickly forgotten. The reasons for failure are many and varied, but common causes include:

- lack of co-ordination of resources and activities
- lack of communication with interested parties, leading to products being delivered that are not what the customer wanted
- poor estimation of time-scales and the costs, leading to projects taking more time and costing more money than expected
- failure to define success criteria and to put in place effective risk management, benefit realisation, monitoring and evaluation arrangements
- inadequate planning of resources, activities and scheduling
- lack of control over progress, so that projects do not reveal their exact status until too late
- lack of quality control, resulting in the delivery of products that are unacceptable or unusable
- failure to undertake robust risk analysis.

A good project management method will guide the project through a controlled, well-managed, visible set of activities to achieve the desired results. The recommended methodology within the public sector is PRINCE (**PR**ojects **IN** **C**ontrolled **E**nvironment), which is now a de facto standard in wide use within the UK.

PRINCE adopts the principles of good project management to avoid the problems outlined above. These principles are:

- a project is a finite process with a definite start and end date
- a project always need to be managed in order to be successful
- for genuine commitment to the project, all parties must be clear about why the project is needed, what it is designed to deliver, how the outcomes are to be achieved, and a clear definition of roles and responsibilities.

Overview

This section of the business case should address the issues listed below. Each issue is explained, together with the process for delivering the required outcomes.

- the procurement strategy
- the project methodology and structure
- the project plan
- use of advisors
- contract management
- benefits realisation
- risk management
- post-project evaluation

The procurement strategy

The procurement strategy focuses on how best the required services and outputs can be procured. Strategic considerations typically range from whether the organisation should act as a single entity or procure collaboratively (perhaps with the parent organisation or a strategic business partner), to the method of procurement to be adopted.

Collaborative procurements are now increasingly commonplace on account of strategic and VFM considerations. In the context of the former, a business driver within the public sector is currently more joined-up government, through adoption of the e-commerce agenda. Consequently, two departments of state with complementary business activities and similar stakeholders and clients might procure together in order to achieve this policy objective and take advantage of economies of scale in the process. An example of such an arrangement might conceivably apply to the Inland Revenue and Customs, both of whom are in the revenue collection business.

Similarly, in the private sector, a parent company might seek to rationalise its business operations and achieve economies of scale and lower costs through collaborative procurements on behalf of its constituent companies.

Alternatively, in the NHS, such an arrangement might be based on geographic considerations: all health providers within a regional area may choose to collaborate in support of an NHS objective, such as the creation of the Electronic Health Record (EHR) – a single electronic record of a client's health history from cradle to grave.

Method of procurement

Choices range from single tender to competitive procurements, involving a variety of procurement routes. Single tender may be the preferred choice for relatively low-value procurements, where the services or the supplies to be procured are reasonably well defined and the market price(s), within certain tolerances, fairly well known and stable. The time-scale within which items need to be procured for operational reasons might also be a key determinant. However, where these criteria do not apply, it may be advantageous to undertake a competitive procurement.

In the case of the public sector, where there is an obligation to procure competitively, choices might involve:

- the use of framework agreements, whereby potential service providers and suppliers have already been competitively selected for reasonably straightforward and standard supplies and services
- advertising within the OJEC, in accordance with EC/WTO Regulations.

The key to a successful procurement strategy is to select a procurement method and route that is manageable (in terms of its complexity), achievable (in terms of time-scale) and will deliver VFM (in terms of competitive forces). Chapter 9 provides guidance on how to manage the procurement process to secure the desired outcome.

A timetable for the procurement should be defined from the outset. This should be kept under regular review. In the case of a major capital scheme (say procurement of a new hospital with 650 beds), a typical example of the likely procurement timetable is provided in Table 7.1.

Table 7.1: Procurement timetable for a major new build scheme

Milestone	To be completed by
Develop and agree SOC	December 2000 (assumes 2 months)
Submission and approval of OBC	April 2001
Completion of public consultation	May 2001
Confirmation of outline planning permission	June 2001
Output specification agreed	July 2001
ITN and information memorandum agreed	August 2001
OJEC notice placed	September 2001
Pre-qualification and long list	December 2001
Issue preliminary ITN	December 2001
Short list and issue ITN	February 2002
Receive priced bids and evaluate bids	May 2002
Negotiations and BAFO	July 2002
Preferred bidder selected	August 2002
FBC submitted and approved	November 2002
Financial close	January 2003
Start on site	March 2003
Facility up and running	April 2005

Project methodology and structure

Most large organisations now have project-management methodologies in place, which are based on their perceived standards of best practice and quality management principles. As noted before, the standard approach to project management in the public sector is PRINCE. This method is also being increasingly adopted by the private sector.

PRINCE covers the project life cycle from start-up to closure. It provides a number of mechanisms and reporting arrangements to ensure project planning and monitoring are carried out rigorously. It is important to ensure that the project managers are properly trained in the PRINCE methodology. Indeed, the economic appraisal should make explicit allowance for project management in the widest sense, i.e. resources for the management of risks, benefit realisation, contract management, monitoring and post-project evaluation.

Project structure

As a minimum, the project structure will generally comprise of the project board, the project manager and project team. Roles, responsibilities and levels of designated authority should be clearly defined from the outset.

The project board is responsible for the overall direction and management of the project and, in particular, the commitment of resources to the project, such as personnel, cash and equipment. Other key responsibilities include vetting and approving all deliverables – project initiation document (PID), risk-logs, mid-stage and end-stage assessments, project closure, etc.

The seniority of the membership of the project board will be dependent on the importance, size and likely cost of the project. For large, complex and risky projects, it is important for the organisation's board members to be represented on the project board.

PRINCE mandates that the project board must represent three broad interests. These include:

- executive role to represent the business perspective
- senior user role to represent the interests of end users or customers
- senior supplier to represent the technical perspective or supply-side interests.

The project manager oversees the day-to-day management of the project. He or she should be appointed for the whole duration of the project. Key responsibilities include:

- ensuring the project progresses to time and budget
- maintaining the risk-log
- managing interfaces with other projects
- reporting to the project board
- initiating any corrective actions necessary to deliver the project successfully.

The project manager's role also includes the management of the project team. The composition of the team itself will depend on the required activities within the project plan.

Quality assurance should be built into the structure of the project from the outset. The project assurance role includes responsibility for monitoring all aspects of the project's performance vis-à-vis the agreed outputs. This task needs to be undertaken by someone who is independent. It is not appropriate for this role to be fulfilled by the project manager.

By way of an example, Figure 7.1 depicts the project team structure which will be put in place to deliver the new hospital we referred to in Table 7.1 above. Their main responsibilities are also indicated.

The project board in this case includes representation from the organisation's main board, the main commissioner of its services and the lead service provider. They encompass the following:

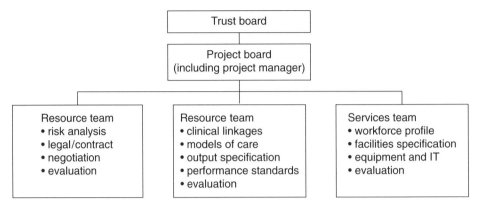

Figure 7.1: Project team structure.

- chairman
- non-executive director
- chief executive (SRO)
- director of finance and performance management
- medical director
- director of nursing
- director of human resources
- director from the health authority
- director from the project company (service provider)
- full-time project manager.

Project plan

The project plan is a document that describes how, when and by whom a specific target or sets of targets is to be achieved. In other words, it is a design of how identified targets for deliverables, time-scales, costs and quality can be achieved.

The project plan should be summarised in the business case, and should address the following criteria:

- the deliverables (or products) to be produced
- the activities required to deliver them
- the activities required to validate the quality of the deliverables
- the resource and time needed for all activities and any need for people with specific skills and capabilities
- the dependencies between activities and any associated constraints

- when activities will occur
- the points at which progress will be monitored, controlled and reviewed.

It is helpful to supplement the description of the project plan with a suitable diagram. Typically, project plans are illustrated by means of a Gantt Chart. Microsoft Project is ideal for this purpose.

Use of advisors

The project plan may have indicated the need for external support and expertise, particularly in the case of large complex projects or – in the case of smaller organisations – where the relevant expertise does not exist.

Specialist advice can generally be categorised into four main types: financial, legal, technical and project management. The project management case should indicate when and how this advice will be utilised, together with expected costs.

Preparing forecasts for the use of external advisors is particularly important, given their relatively high cost and their poor deployment within many procurements to date. The guide produced by the Treasury Taskforce Guide (*How to Appoint and Manage Advisors*) provides practical tips on how to make effective use of advisors. It also addresses charging mechanisms for incentivising advisors to deliver the required outputs.

Contract management arrangements

An integral part of the project management case is sound arrangements for managing the contract. The case should summarise the approach and resources in place for management of the contract.

It is important to establish the management arrangements before the contract is awarded. This allows monitoring of the performance of the contract to begin from the outset.

The guidance contained in the NHS Executive's Capital Investment Manual remains valid for the management of traditional, public sector procurements. Bespoke guidance for PFI procurements has been produced by the Treasury Task Force – *How to Manage the Delivery of Long Term PFI Contracts, 2000*.

It is important that responsibility for managing the contract, whether traditional or PFI, is vested in appropriately skilled personnel. Failure to manage the contract effectively will lead to a number of undesirable outcomes:

- non-delivery of the contracted services
- failure to realise whatever VFM was inherent in the deal at the contract negotiation stage
- lack of an objective basis for authorising service payments and applying sanctions in the case of poor performance of the contractor
- failure to manage risk — including danger of assuming risk which the contractor is paid to manage
- inability to develop an effective long-term partnership with the contractor.

PFI contracts can span up to 30 years. It is impossible to plan for everything that may impact adversely on the project over this period. It is, therefore, important for the right type of relationship to be developed with the contractor. The right balance must be struck between a hands-on and a hands-off approach to monitoring the contract. Too much hands-on monitoring can make it difficult, if not impossible, for the contractor to perform its side of the deal.

It is also important to develop suitable change control mechanisms, exception reporting and provision for resolution of disputes. Clear, simple, transparent, fair and auditable systems must also be developed with the contractor to support the monitoring of the contract. Over-complex systems are likely to be costly to implement and difficult to enforce. Information-intensive procedures should also be avoided. The systems are more likely to be effective if they are jointly developed with the contractor.

The end of the contraction duration should also feature in the plan. What will be the respective roles and responsibilities of the parties at this stage? Will there be a need for re-competition? Is there a requirement for the contractor to handover the asset to the client? What are the available options at this point?

Long-term partnerships require time, energy, effort and mutual trust to maintain momentum and meet contractual obligations without resort to litigation and other heavy-handed measures. Allowance should also be made for change of contract managers which will have an impact on the ongoing relationship. Suitable succession plans and hand-over arrangements should be developed.

Benefits realisation arrangements

Experience has shown that the benefits which underlie the economic appraisal are seldomly realised in full. This is largely a result of the failure to develop effective benefit realisation arrangements at the outset of the

Table 7.2: Benefit realisation framework

Benefit reference no.	Should be cross-referenced to the economic appraisal
Description of benefit	Reduced clerical workload in pay unit
System feature	Integrated purchase order and payments system
Potential dis-benefits	None
Activities needed to secure benefit	Reorganise payments procedures, distribute purchase order and goods received notification to managers
Responsible officer	Director of finance and information
Performance measure	Number of payments clerk in post
Target improvements	Reduce from 3 to 1 staff
Full-year value	£15,000
Time-scale	Years 2–3

project. The project management case should summarise the benefit realisation plan which will be used to manage delivery of the expected benefits.

For each benefit assessed in the economic appraisal, an effective benefit realisation plan should address the following issues in a systematic manner:

- provide a clear description of the benefit
- indicate what aspect of the project will give rise to the benefit to facilitate monitoring
- indicate any potential dis-benefits
- record the activities needed to secure the benefit
- state who is responsible for delivering the benefit
- specify a suitable performance indicator or measure for tracking the benefit
- specify the target improvement or expected level of change
- specify the expected full-year value of the benefit
- specify the time-scale for realisation of the benefit.

It is also recommended that a detailed benefits register is used in addition to an overarching benefits realisation plan. An example of a benefit realisation plan for an IS/IT investment, based on the above framework, is provided in Table 7.2.

Risk-management strategy

This section of the project management case should highlight the risk-management strategy for the project. In particular, it should reference relevant organisational policies and frameworks for the ongoing management and control of risks, including those which will arise specifically from the proposed investment.

A good risk-management strategy should exhibit the following characteristics:

- All risks should be identified, classified and assessed before considering how they should be managed.
- The allocation of risk should reflect the principle of optimum transfer: which party is best placed to control the probability and/or impact of the risk?
- Risk management needs to be continuous and kept up to date.
- A suitable contingency plan should be developed to deal with the worst eventuality.
- Risk management should be integrated into the organisation's daily operations and should not be complicated or burdensome.
- Explicit allowance should be made for the skills and resources needed to implement the risk management system.
- Roles and responsibilities should be made clear, especially in contracts where some risks have been transferred to other parties.

A key output from the risk assessment work is production of a risk allocation matrix (RAM). There are four main stages in producing a RAM:

- Identification stage – list all known risks associated with the project.
- Evaluation and quantification stage – assess the likelihood and impact of each risk on a scale of low, medium and high. Where information and experience are available, quantify all risks which are inherently quantifiable.
- Allocation stage – allocate risks between the parties depending on their ability to manage the risks.
- Management stage – manage all risks that are retained by the public sector once the package of risks has been apportioned between the parties.

In PFI contracts, the public sector should concentrate on managing those risks it has retained. Its risk-management strategy should detail how it plans to minimise these risks and what action will be taken if problems do occur.

This should be considered alongside the benefit realisation plan. Ultimately, the main risks relate to non-delivery or late delivery of the expected benefits from the investment.

It is also important to ensure the contractor has a robust strategy for managing all risks which have been transferred before the contract is awarded. Smith (1999), Chapter 4, addresses risk management requirements within the context of PFI projects in detail. In general, design, construction and operating risks (cost, time and performance) should be transferred to the private sector in PFI schemes. The degree of transfer of other risks is subject to negotiation, taking into account the respective capacities of the parties to control the risks.

Post-project evaluation

Arrangements for evaluation of the project during the formative and summative stages need to be put in place in accordance with best practice. The arrangements should be summarised in the project management case. Vague statements of intent should be avoided.

Lack of commitment to post-project evaluation is a major weakness in public sector projects. Partly as a result of the one-off nature of major capital investments within the career span of the average senior manager, there are no effective sanctions for not complying with the requirement for post-project evaluation. Yet without regular and rigorous evaluations, it is difficult to learn lessons and improve the way projects are designed and improved over time. Ultimately, the corporate knowledge of the public sector is seriously eroded and VFM from scarce public resources is undermined.

Commitment to evaluation should be secured from senior management and the board. It is important for evaluation to be regarded as an integral part of the management of the project.

As a minimum, the evaluation framework should summarise:

- purpose of the evaluation
- key issues which will be addressed (it is important for this to reflect the design of the preferred option in the economic appraisal, including issues relating to costs, benefits, risks and underlying assumptions)
- summary of the data collection methods
- timing of the evaluation (both formative and summative evaluation)
- resources set aside for evaluation
- roles and responsibilities for undertaking the evaluation
- dissemination strategy for ensuring the results of the evaluation are used to inform the performance of the project or subsequent projects within or across the organisation.

To ensure that evaluation is conducted systematically and is tied directly to the original economic appraisal, some departments and agencies, most notably the Department for Education and Employment, have developed what is known as the ROAMEF framework:

- **R**ationale (i.e. what is the justification for the project? How is it intended to alter the status quo?)
- **O**bjectives (i.e. what are the objectives and how do they complement the rationale? Are they defined in SMART terms to facilitate assessment of their achievement?)
- **A**ppraisal (i.e. what options have been considered to meet the objectives? What is the preferred option?)
- **M**onitoring (i.e. how will progress against the stated objectives be monitored? What monitoring information and supporting systems are required for this purpose?)
- **E**valuation (i.e. what plans are in place to assess the impact of the project while it is in progress or after it has been completed? Has the project delivered what it set out to achieve? Have outcomes been achieved in line with the estimates provided in the business case?)
- **F**eedback (i.e. what plans are in place to ensure the lessons from the evaluation are used to inform future project design, planning, implementation and management?).

Conclusion

The key points from this chapter may be summarised as follows.

- An effective project management case is crucial to successful delivery of the desired outcomes from the project.
- Consideration should be given to the procurement strategy from the outset.
- The preparation of plans for the scoping, procurement, implementation and operational phases of the project, and the continuous monitoring and review of these plans, is essential throughout the project.
- Most organisations have a project management methodology. This should be used and tailored to the specific requirements of each procurement. It is essential, however, to build the business, user and

technical perspectives into the project team and to take on board the requirement for third-party assurance (independent quality reviews).

- Specialist, external advisors will be required for complex, novel and risky projects. They are an expensive resource which should be used efficiently and effectively. Ensure support is commissioned at the right stage.
- Effective arrangements for the management of services (contract management), the delivery of benefits (benefits realisation plan) and the mitigation of associated risks (risk management strategy) must be put in place from the outset.
- Systematic monitoring and evaluation of the project must be undertaken. The evaluation must be conducted against the estimates for costs, benefits and risks recorded in the original economic appraisal.
- The lessons from the evaluation should be used to inform the project or the way future projects are designed, implemented and managed.

PART THREE

The production process

CHAPTER EIGHT

Tools and techniques for capital investment appraisal

This chapter provides an exposition on the essential tools and techniques for capital investment appraisal. It also summarises the strengths and weaknesses of the various approaches on offer, including pitfalls to avoid. Worked examples are provided to aid readers' understanding of key concepts and principles.

Introduction

HM Treasury's 'Green Book' makes clear that investment is not a 'standard drill' but a flexible, systematic approach to expenditure proposals. In broad terms, an appraisal is characterised by the following steps:

- clear statement of investment objectives
- identification of options
- assessment of costs, benefits and risks for each short-listed option
- adjust costs and benefits for the time value of money where appropriate
- weigh up the uncertainties
- assess other factors which have a bearing on the decision-making process
- present the results and recommend a preferred option.

Our experience of reviewing and producing business cases throws up a number of weaknesses in the practice of investment appraisal. The following issues will be addressed in turn:

- methods for investment appraisal
- rationale for discounting
- valuing costs and benefits
- what cash flows to include
- appraisal period
- public sector comparators
- sensitivity analysis
- risk analysis.

Methods for investment appraisal – accounting-based and economics-based

There are two main schools of thought for evaluating the financial performance of an investment project, namely 'accounting methods' and 'economics methods'. The former focuses on liquidity/payback period and profitability, while the latter is more concerned with wealth maximisation, cash flows, resource allocation, and considerations of risk and uncertainty.

Common examples of accounting-based methods of investment appraisal are payback period and return on capital employed. The two main economics-based methods are net present value (NPV) and internal rate of return.

Payback period

As implied by the term, this method measures the rate at which the benefits from the investment 'pays back' the initial investment costs. In general, projects with a short payback period are preferable to those with long payback periods. This is particularly the case if the investor faces major liquidity problems.

Box 8.1: An example of payback period

Consider two projects with the following cash-flow projections:

Project A

Year	Costs	Benefits
0	−£10,000	0
1	0	3000
2	0	5000
3	**0**	**2000**
4	0	7000

Project B

Year	Costs	Benefits
0	−£8000	0
1	0	3000
2	**0**	**5000**
3	0	2000
4	0	1000

Project B would be preferred because the investment costs are recouped after three years compared with four years for project A.

Weaknesses

One obvious advantage of this method is its simplicity. However, it suffers from a number of weaknesses:

- It uses 'speed of return' rather than 'rate of return' as the basis for investment appraisal.
- It has a 'short-term' bias.
- It does not recognise the time value of money.
- It does not take the full economic life of the investment into account. Cash flows outside the 'desired payback period' are ignored, thus creating the potential to make sub-optimal decisions.
- The cut-off point for the payback period and decision rule is arbitrary.

To overcome the first weakness, some managers adopt the 'discounted payback' approach. This simply discounts the future cash flows by an appropriate discount rate to express the figures in present value. Although this is an improvement on the basic payback method, the other weaknesses still remain.

Return on capital employed (ROCE)

This method is also known as the 'accounting rate of return', 'return on book value' and 'return on investment'. It is calculated as the ratio of the accounting profit arising from the investment to the required capital outlay, and is expressed in percentage terms.

As with all investment appraisal methods, it requires a decision rule. Senior managers within the organisation would stipulate a minimum acceptable ROCE or 'hurdle rate' for any investment proposal. In setting the hurdle rate, managers would take the prevailing rate of return for the organisation as a whole into account. For mutually exclusive projects, the one with the highest ROCE and which satisfies the hurdle rate would be preferred.

Despite its intuitive appeal, this method suffers from some of the same weaknesses present in the payback method. Both methods can result in sub-optimal decisions.

It ignores the time value of money. In addition, it suffers from measurement difficulties, partly on account of its different variants. Disagreement abounds on how 'capital employed' and 'profit' should be calculated. For example, profit can be calculated net of financing expenses, tax and depreciation or can be computed in gross terms. This method is based on 'accounting profit' rather than 'cash flows' or resource costs and benefits.

Attributes of a sound appraisal method: net present value

A sound investment appraisal method:

- focuses on cash flows rather than on 'accounting measures' of financial success
- recognises the time value of money
- recognises the full life of the investment rather than focusing on a subset of the cash flows
- takes risk into account
- is driven by a clear, objective decision-making rule.

The NPV method exhibits all these features. It compares the present value of the future cash inflows (discounted benefits) with the cash outflows (the discounted costs). If the NPV is greater than zero, the investment should be accepted. If there are mutually exclusive projects, the decision rule is to accept the project with the highest positive NPV.

To apply this method, you need to know the following:

- the amount of capital required for the investment ('initial outlay')
- the future cash flows arising from the investment
- the life-span of the investment
- the relevant discount rate (ideally a risk-adjusted discount rate).

See Table 8.2 for a worked example of the NPV method and Appendix 3 for the key components of the NPV method.

Discounting

Given the importance of 'discounting' to correct application of the NPV method, a brief exposition on discounting is in order. When comparing cash flows which occur at different points in time, it is important to make allowance for 'the time value of money'. 'Jam today is worth more than jam tomorrow', so the cash flows need to be reduced to a common denominator! In economists' parlance, individuals have a positive rate of time preference.

There are a number of reasons for attaching greater weight to earlier costs and benefits than to those occurring later. They include:

- the loss of the opportunity to invest the money and earn a return
- inflation, which has the effect of eroding the value of money
- risk and uncertainty (including ill health and death)

- individuals might expect to have greater income and wealth in the future, thus money received today provides more utility than money received when they are richer.

Discounting is the process of adjusting cash flows arising at different periods to a common currency, namely, their 'present value'. The discount rate indicates the rate at which the present value of a future value (say a pound for convenience) declines in value over time. It is the converse of compounding interest, which measures the rate at which money invested today will increase over time.

Box 8.2: An example of discounting

Suppose you were to give Naomi £100 today and she decides to invest it in a building society account for one year at a 10% interest rate. At the end of this period, she will receive £110. We say that the 'present value' of £110 received in one year's time is £100. The 10% is the 'discount rate'. It measures the rate at which money declines in value over time. It is the rate of return which is needed to compensate Naomi to forgo the immediate use of her £100.

The formula for compounding and discounting may be expressed as follows:

Let F = future value of a cash flow
  P = present value of a cash flow
  i = interest rate
  N = number of years for the cash flow

The formula for compounding (i.e. to find the future value of the investment) is $F = P * (1 + i)^n$. Thus the future value of Naomi's investment is £100 * (1 + 0.10) which gives £110.

If we solve for P, this gives the formula for discounting (i.e. the present value of the future cash flows):

$$P = \frac{F}{(1 + i)^n}$$

Thus the £110 which Naomi receives after one year is worth £100 in today's money (i.e. £110/(1 + 0.10))

There is an inverse relationship between the present value of a cash flow and the discount rate used in the discounting process. This is illustrated in Table 8.1. The present value also decreases the further into the future the money is received.

Table 8.1: Present value of £1 (extract)

Year	Interest rate (% per annum)			
	6	8	10	15
1	0.9434	0.9259	0.9091	0.8696
2	0.8900	0.8573	0.8264	0.7561
3	0.8396	0.7938	0.7513	0.6575
4	0.7921	0.7350	0.6830	0.5718
5	0.7473	0.6806	0.6209	0.4972
10	0.5584	0.4632	0.3855	0.2472

Example: application of NPV

Consider a basic project with cash flows as follows (initial capital outlay of £4000 and savings of £2000 for the second, third and fourth year, and a scrap value of £1700). Assume the cost of capital is 6% and the life span of the project is 5 years. Is this project worth undertaking?

Table 8.2: A worked example of NPV

Year	Cash-flow items	Undiscounted cash flows	Discount factor	Discounted cash flow
0	Initial capital outlay	(−)£4000	1	(−)£4000
1	Saving	£2000	0.9434	£1887
2	Saving	£1000	0.8900	£890
3	Saving	£500	0.8396	£420
4	Residual value	£1700	0.7921	£1347
Net present value		£1200		£544

Other things being equal, the project should be accepted since its has a positive NPV. The present value of the benefits outweighs the present value of the costs by £544. Of course, there may be other factors which are material to the decision making which may not be fully reflected in the figures included in the appraisal.

This may include costs and benefits which cannot easily be quantified in monetary values. Typical examples are improvements in staff morale, improved access to services and suffering from accidents. If reliable values can be imputed for these costs and benefits, this can be legitimately factored in the appraisal. Otherwise, they should be weighted and scored and presented separately, alongside the results of the discounted cash-flow analysis.

Internal rate of return (IRR)

The IRR method shares many of the features of the NPV method. It is also based on discounted cash flows. This method approaches the investment decision from the perspective of estimating what the rate of return would have to be to make the NPV zero. All projects with an IRR greater than the company's cost of capital would be considered to be attractive. For example, if the IRR is 40% and the company's opportunity cost of capital is 15%, this would be considered to be a very profitable proposal. Conversely, if the IRR was less than 15%, the project would not be accepted in this case.

The calculation of the IRR is not straightforward. It requires guessing, trial and error! A common approach is to use 'interpolation'. You would choose two discount rates, one rate that gives a positive NPV and one that yields a negative NPV, and interpolate the IRR which would necessarily lie between the two discount rates selected. Note that as the discount rate of the investment increases, the NPV will decrease. Formulas are also built into Lotus and Excel spreadsheets to calculate the IRR, but you would still have to input your best guess for the value of the IRR leaving the computer to iterate until it generates an accurate answer.

There are a number of technical pitfalls to avoid when using the IRR method. These include the possibility of multiple IRRs, problems in ranking and choosing between mutually exclusive projects of different scale, and the possibility of different opportunity cost of capital in the short-term and long-term, thus making it difficult to compare the project's IRR with 'the' opportunity cost of capital.

NPV: the winner

On account of the limitations with these three methods for appraising capital projects, the approach recommended for public sector projects is the NPV method. This method is capable of providing consistently reliable solutions. However, considerable care should be taken in setting up the discounted cash-flow model and assembling the base inputs.

Key issues to consider when applying the NPV method include the choice of the discount rate, the length of the appraisal horizon, the treatment of inflation, uncertainty, risk and intangible costs and benefits which are inherently difficult to quantify (for detailed guidance see Chapters 4 and 5 of Smith, 1999).

Valuing costs and benefits

Costs and benefits should be valued at prices which reflect their opportunity costs (i.e. their value in the next-best alternative use). For example,
if an NHS organisation decides to build a hospital on land which it owns,
this land has a market value (i.e. an opportunity cost) which should be
factored into the investment appraisal as a cost.

In cases where market prices are distorted on account of 'market failures'
(e.g. monopoly power) or where there are no markets for a particular input
or output, considerable care needs to be exercised in the valuation process
to avoid biased assessments. A number of approaches have been developed
to value non-marketed goods. These include:

- revealed preference approach (i.e. inferring a price from consumers'
  behaviour)
- willingness to pay (i.e. imputing a price by means of carefully constructed questionnaires and interviews to indicate how much people are
  prepared to pay to consume a particular output – say improved access
  to services or savings in time – or to avoid an undesirable outcome).

The values obtained from the willingness-to-pay approach will vary between
individuals, depending on their income, socioeconomic status and personal
circumstances.

Within the health sector, one widely accepted variant of the willingness-
to-pay approach for valuing health outcomes is 'quality-adjusted life year'
(QALY). The numeraire in this case is quantity of life (reduced mortality)
and quality gains (reduced morbidity), rather than money.

QALYs take into account individuals' preferences for the different health
states, where 1 is taken to mean 'perfect health' and 0 denotes death. The
quality-adjusted weight for each health state is multiplied by the time in
the state and then summed to estimate the number of QALYs. This figure
(a measure of health outcomes) can be combined with the relevant costs
of the particular programme or treatment option to produce a cost per
QALY gained. Health economists term this type of evaluation 'cost-utility
analysis'. As with other types of evaluation, future effects may also be discounted, and discounted at an appropriate rate (see Drummond *et al.*, 1999).

Weighting and scoring

If there are no generally accepted methods for valuing project outputs,
weighting and scoring approaches may be used to quantify these impacts.
This is done in three stages. In stage one, you identify the benefits in

question and attach weights to them to reflect their relative importance. The weights should sum to 100%.

In stage 2, you score each option even-handedly against the benefit criteria in question. The scoring system needs to be clear. For computational ease, it is standard practice to score the options on a scale of 0 to 10, where 0 denotes that the option does not contribute at all to the benefit in question. A score of 10 denotes that the option has the potential to deliver all of the benefit in question.

In stage 3, you multiply the weight by the score to yield a total weighted score for each option. Ignoring cost and risks from the equation for the time being, the higher the total weighted score, the more attractive is the particular option.

The total weighted score for each option may be combined with the net present costs of each option to provide a measure of the cost-effectiveness of each option. A simple measure of cost-effectiveness is to divide the net present cost estimate for each option with its corresponding total weighted score to produce a cost per benefit point estimate. Other things being equal, the lower the cost per benefit point, the more attractive is the particular option.

The process and reasoning behind the scores and weights must be clearly recorded. It is the number of people involved in the process; their expertise and the manner in which the assessment is conducted which lends credibility to this method of assessment. It is important to involve the right people and conduct the process fairly and objectively.

Areas of doubt should be recorded. These should be tested via suitable sensitivity analysis. The sensitivity analysis should explore whether plausible changes in the weights and scores change the ranking of the options. Sensitivity analysis is discussed later in this chapter.

Sunk costs

These are costs that have already been incurred or are already irrevocably committed. All such costs should be excluded as they are bygones and not material to the present decision. Examples of this are money spent on feasibility studies, pilots or pre-project survey work.

Inflation

Both the discount rate and cash flows must be expressed in the same terms, either real or nominal. The former excludes inflation while the latter includes inflation. It should be noted that the standard discount rate stipulated by HM Treasury (currently 6%) is a real test discount rate (TDR). The cash flows for use with this TDR should similarly be expressed in real terms. Note that using real cash flows with a real TDR will normally yield the same results as using nominal cash flows with a nominal discount rate.

In cases where inflation has the same impact on the cash flows for the options under consideration, it is customary to compute all costs and benefits at the prevailing price level in the year in which the appraisal is undertaken (i.e. the 'base year'), rather than adding the inflation factor to the TDR and respective cash flows. However, if some cash flows are likely to be significantly out of line with the general rate of inflation, the differential should be reflected in the calculation. For example, in the case of a building project, construction costs tend to increase at a faster rate than say labour costs. If we assume that the price of building materials increases at 3.5% per annum and the other costs increase by the general rate of inflation (say 2% for ease of illustration), the difference which should be added to building materials costs is 1.5%. Once this adjustment has been made, the figures should be discounted by the prevailing real TDR.

$$\text{Nominal discount rate} = [(1 + \text{real rate}) \times (1 + \text{inflation rate})] - 1$$

$$\text{Real discount rate} = \frac{(1 + \text{nominal rate})}{(1 + \text{inflation rate})} - 1$$

Discount rate

The discount rate for use in appraisal of public sector projects is often termed the 'test discount rate' (TDR) and is stipulated by HM Treasury. The current rate is set at 6% in real terms and is chosen to reflect the opportunity cost of public sector capital and the social rate of time preference. The latter is a measure of society's willingness to forego consumption today in order to enjoy more consumption at a future date.

Other rates may be appropriate, subject to clearance from HM Treasury, where:

- there is exceptional systematic risk
- discounting extends to the very long term (say beyond 50 years)
- the cash flows are nominal
- time preference for income or public expenditure is not relevant to the project in question.

Base year 'Year 0'

The normal practice is to take the mid-point of the year in which the appraisal is conducted as the base date (Year 0). Subsequent years extending to the life of the contract and/or the life span of the investment should be treated as years 1, 2, 3 . . . n. Cash flows should reflect the years in which they arise. The year chosen for the base date should be clearly indicated in the appraisal.

Projects with unequal lives

If two projects or two options for a project have different life spans, their NPVs cannot be compared on a like-for-like basis. One approach to comparing the options fairly is the use of equivalent annual cash flows or costs (EAC).

This is simply the NPV of the projects divided by the relevant annuity factor:

$$EAC = \text{net present value/annuity factor for n years at i\%.}$$

Box 8.3: An example of projects with unequal lives

Consider two projects with the following characteristics. Project A has a life span of 6 years and an NPV of £40,000 while project B has a life span of 3 years and an NPV of £35,000. Let us assume that both projects are discounted at 16%. This gives rise to an annuity factor of 3.6847 for project A and 2.2469 for project B.

The respective EACs of the projects are:

Project A = £40,000/3.6847 = £10,856

Project B = £35,000/2.2469 = £15,577.

The project which yields the higher equivalent annual cash flow (i.e. project B) is preferred as it delivers the greatest return on the investment.

Alternatively, if the benefits are the same, the decision rule is to choose the project with the lowest EAC.

Depreciation and capital charges

Depreciation should be omitted from the appraisal. It is a process of apportioning the capital costs over the life of the project. The NPV method is an economics-based approach which handles capital costs in an alternative way by reducing all costs and benefits to a single point in time. The two methods should not be confused.

Ignore all financing charges (interest charges, dividends, etc.), as these are already addressed through the discounting process. Otherwise, there will be double counting of resources.

Transfer payments

Transfer payments are payments for which no good or service is obtained in return. Non-resource cash flows should be excluded from the economic appraisal as they do not increase the 'wealth of the nation'. A typical example is VAT, which transfers money from one part of the public sector to another.

Wider costs and benefits

Costs and benefits should be assessed from the perspective of the wider public sector rather than being restricted to the organisation which initiates the project. The wider consequential impact of the investment options must be assessed. For example, a project to build or extend a motorway will create costs and benefits for public sector organisations other than the Department of Environment, Transport and the Regions. The effects will also fall on the private sector. All these direct and indirect consequences of the investment should be appraised and recorded in the business case.

Appraisal period

Projects should normally be appraised over their expected life span. This will obviously vary from project to project. For new-build schemes in the health sector, for example, the normal practice is to appraise the option over 60 years. This is assumed to be the life span of a new hospital building. As these are purpose-built facilities with limited opportunities for alternative use in a 'second-hand' market, it is standard practice to further assume that the public sector would utilise the asset until it is fully depreciated or requires a major refurbishment or redevelopment. Allowance should obviously be made for the costs of ongoing maintenance to keep the asset in a fit for purpose state.

If a refurbishment is proposed during the physical life span of the project, an appraisal should be made to weigh up the relative merits of refurbishment, disposal or leaving the asset in its current state.

In the case of privately financed hospital schemes, the normal practice is to appraise PFI options over both the primary lease or contract period (typically 30 years) and 60 years (the assumed life span of the asset). Equivalent annual costs should be computed to facilitate a valid comparison between the public sector comparator option (60 years) and the PFI option with the reduced life span (30 years). For the extended PFI option, the financial model used by the Special Purpose Vehicle may be used to estimate the costs beyond the primary contract period. Both the PFI option and the publicly funded alternative should be tailored to the same output specification throughout the 60-year period. All assumptions should be made explicit and tested in the risk and sensitivity analysis.

Information technology projects will have considerably shorter life spans before they require a major refresh. Conventionally, such projects are assumed to have a life span of 7 years.

As projects will vary in their life spans and economic life (i.e. the point at which a major refresh or refurbishment is required), a safe generalisation is to appraise over the expected duration of the contract with service providers. This is particularly the case with projects financed under the PFI.

It is important to reflect the whole-life cost of the project in the appraisal. This includes the initial capital costs, operating or revenue costs (such as maintenance and staffing), decanting costs, wider consequential costs on other sectors and any resulting opportunity costs (e.g. value of land or other assets tied up in the project). In some cases, there may be a positive residual value (a benefit) if the economic life of the asset exceeds the life of the project. This should also be addressed in the economic appraisal.

If there are uncertainties about the physical or useful life of the asset and any of the underlying costs and benefits, sensitivity analysis should be performed to assess the impact of these parameters on the base results.

Public sector comparators

As explained in Chapter 4, the 'preferred option' identified prior to the commencement of the tendering process has an important role to play in gauging VFM once bids are subsequently received from the marketplace.

The PSC provides an estimate of how much it would cost the public sector, as a traditional supplier, to provide the facility and associated services defined in the output specification for the project. In its formative stages, the PSC is often referred to as the *reference project*, since it acts as a reference point for affordability at an early stage.

To facilitate a fair comparison with bids from suppliers, it is important for the PSC to be calculated on a basis consistent with that used to assess suppliers' bids. In particular, it should make explicit allowance for risks that are retained by the public sector under this option. It should also be tailored to the same output-based specification as suppliers' bids, in terms of both quantity and quality of services. This does not mean the public sector should emulate the private sector's solution. Rather, the public sector should not attempt to manipulate the outcome of the VFM test by deliberately adopting ineffective and inefficient solutions which do not reflect recent construction and management practices in the public sector.

Occasionally, it may be possible to estimate the cost of the PSC or reference project assuming a PFI structure. But generally this will only be in circumstances where it has been decided, first, that a privately financed solution is the only way forward (as in the case of HM Treasury *Significant PFI (PPP) Projects*); and, second, costs are available for similar projects (as in the case, say, of PFI new-build hospitals). In the majority of cases, the PSC will be predicated on in-house or outsourced costs for the provision of services, regardless of whether a privately financed solution is still being considered. See also Treasury Taskforce, 2000.

Sensitivity analysis

Uncertainty in investment appraisals is frequently addressed by performing sensitivity analysis on the uncertain parameters. It involves three basic steps:

- Identify the variables which have uncertain values.
- Specify the plausible range for the variables in question and state the reason for the range specified. Arbitrariness in the selected range should be avoided! Expert opinion or evidence should be sought.
- Compute results under pessimistic scenario, most likely scenario and optimistic scenario. Avoid simplistic one-way sensitivity analysis. In practice, more than one of the uncertain parameters are likely to vary at the same time.

Typical parameters to vary include the main capital costs, operating costs, estimates of savings, time horizons for the investment and all assumptions which have a major impact on the choice of preferred option.

Box 8.4: Health warning from Neil Bruce Copp, Chairman of the Winner Foundation and the Founder of the Targus Empire

Eliminating optimistic bias and undertaking some form of sensitivity analysis, however crude, is key to deciding whether an investment proposal is likely to be affordable and should go ahead. To illustrate the point, in the words of Neil Bruce Copp, Chairman of the Winner Foundation and the founder of Targus, the hugely successful international luggage company:

When I am presented with an investment opportunity – for example, the business plan for a new start-up company – my final decision is based on halving the forecast for the first year's sales turnover and doubling the forecast of associated overhead or running costs. From my experience, this normally brings the entire picture into reality.

A recent example of this, of course, is the Millennium Dome, where a different decision would have been reached if this benchmark had been applied.

Risk analysis

If good stochastic data are available, formal probability analysis is likely to yield more reliable results than sensitivity analysis. The latter is more amenable to manipulation. The variables and the alternative values selected are subjectively determined. Interpretation of the results of a sensitivity analysis is also arbitrary.

Smith (1999), Chapter 4, presents a number of approaches for evaluating risks. This ranges from simple 'rules of thumb' based on experience to formal Monte Carlo and Latin Hypercube analyses. Some of the main approaches are reviewed below. For the sake of brevity, we exclude some of the more modern approaches from portfolio theory, particularly the Capital Asset Pricing Model (CAPM) in determining the required rates of return for risky projects (*see* Smith 1999, for a discussion of the CAPM).

Risk audit interviews

The identification, assessment and management of risks (especially for large projects and small projects that are novel) requires considerable skill and professional judgement. Risk audit interviews and brainstorming workshops will help to identify the relevant risks, assess any interdependencies between the risks, how they might occur, their likelihood of occurring and the likely financial consequences.

These techniques are at the 'soft' end of the analytical spectrum. They are particularly useful at the SOC stage. At the FBC stage (and to a lesser extent the OBC stage), they should be supplemented with 'hard' techniques such as the statistical techniques described later.

A risk audit interview involves interviews led by an experienced risk manager with key project participants and staff. These interviews are conducted individually, and supplemented by peer group meetings and brainstorming sessions. The group will brainstorm all the risks that apply to the project, after which risks may be grouped under common headings. The facilitator will record and distil from these risks the ones which require further investigation. Box 8.5 shows how the risks may be ranked in terms of their probability and potential impact – high, medium and low. These may subsequently be quantified.

Box 8.5: Ranking risks

High/high: High probability of occurrence and high impact

High/low: High probability of occurrence and low impact

Low/high: Low probability of occurrence and high impact

Low/low: Low probability of occurrence and low impact on the project

---

Rules of thumb

Rules of thumb or heuristics are often used to aid decision making. For example, a financial institution may choose to lend three times a person's salary in considering a mortgage application. These rules provide broad guidelines for managers in decision making. They are often based on expert judgement and experience, and supplemented with other information.

As a preliminary step, an NHS trust could, for example, draw on expert opinion and information from comparable schemes to determine what allowance to make for risk. Given the uncertainty in 'rules of thumb' and difficulties in comparing schemes, estimates derived from this approach should be compared with estimates based on more formal approaches (e.g. probability analysis).

Scenario modelling

Scenario modelling assesses the effect on the success or otherwise of an option of combining different assumptions about the future. A small number of scenarios (typically the optimistic, most likely and pessimistic) is selected and the expected net cost of each investment option is calculated for each of the chosen scenarios.

Each scenario can be tested for sensitivity to changes in key variables. Some key questions to explore under each scenario are:

- Does the ranking of the options change under optimistic and pessimistic assumptions?
- How likely are the best and worse case scenarios to arise?
- What would be the effect on affordability and prices to commissioners of each scenario?
- What would be the effect on VFM of each scenario?

Single-point probability analysis

At its most basic, a risk analysis could consist of an estimate of the cost of each risk occurring, multiplied by a single probability of that risk occurring in a particular year.

For example, the risk of cost overruns of a particular service may be estimated as:

- Annual cost of service   £2m
- Estimated impact of risk of cost overrun   £200,000
- Estimated probability of risk occurring   10%
- Estimated value of risk = £200,000 × 10% = £20,000

Multi-point probability analysis

For any risk, a range of possible outcomes is more likely. An output probability distribution gives a complete picture of the possible outcomes and recognises that some of these outcomes are more likely to occur than others. An 'expected' outcome is the average of all possible outcomes, taking into account their different probabilities.

For example, it is estimated that a particular facility will cost £50m to build. The expected cost associated with construction cost uncertainties could be analysed to give the events and the likelihood of occurring shown in Table 8.3.

In this example, the most likely outcome is that of no extra cost, as this outcome has the highest probability. The expected outcome is the sum of each possible outcome multiplied by its probability, i.e. an extra cost of £2.5m. This would need to be calculated in NPV terms, taking account of the time period over which the risk occurs.

The number of likely outcomes may vary for each different risk. In the example above, it was felt that five outcomes could meaningfully be specified, including one for a cost saving in the project. However, introducing extra outcomes need only be done if they add value to the assessment process.

Table 8.3:   Expected cost of construction project

Possible cost (£m)	Difference from estimated cost (£m)	Estimated probability of event occurring	Risk value (£m)
45	−5	0.1	−0.5
50	0	0.6	0
55	+5	0.1	+0.5
60	+10	0.1	+1.0
65	+15	0.1	+1.5

Monte Carlo simulation

There are a variety of packages available that take the analysis of risk using probability distributions a step further. In general, computer simulations start by generating a series of simple profiles to fit a number of defined cases for each risk (usually three): the worst case (maximum impact), the most likely case (expected impact) and the best case (minimum impact). A limited number of standard profiles are usually available within the software, and in some programmes the input can be in the form of a curve chosen from a standard set.

Monte Carlo simulation is widely available for this sort of analysis, although alternative statistical methods are equally acceptable. In this method, a random value of probability and its associated consequence is selected from the sample profile for each risk in turn and these are then combined to give a total value for the overall project. This procedure is repeated for a large number of iterations. The more iterations, the better the accuracy.

Latin hypercube

Latin hypercube is a recent development in sampling theory, designed to reproduce accurately the input distribution through sampling in fewer iterations compared with the Monte Carlo approach. The distinguishing feature of Latin hypercube sampling is stratification of the input probability distributions. A sample is then chosen from each stratified layer of the input distribution. Sampling is forced to represent values in each layer and is thus forced to recreate the input distribution. Convergence tests show that this method of sampling converges faster on the true distributions compared with Monte Carlo sampling.

Risk assessment in PFI projects

The risk assessment for PFI contracts deserves special prominence. As noted before, the risk transfer objective is inextricably linked to the value for money analysis. The private sector, assumed to be rational agents, will charge a premium for assuming any risks transferred to them by the public sector. This is reflected in the bid price for the project. The premium is only worth paying if it is less than the expected cost of the risk in question to the public sector. Otherwise, it is more cost-effective for the public sector to retain the risk.

To make the right judgement, it is therefore important to supplement the traditional economic appraisal with a quantified risk analysis. The latter should seek to estimate the net present cost of the risks which the public sector retains under both the PSC and the best PFI option on offer. The difference between these two values provides a measure of the net risk transfer from the public to the private sector.

The quality of the thinking that informs the risk analysis is crucial to the validity of the resulting output. The GIGO principle should be remembered in this regard – garbage in garbage out! Some useful issues to consider as a prior step include:

- Is the risk inherently quantifiable? If not, qualitative approaches should be employed to assess the risk.
- What is the likely timing of the risk? Is it a one-off risk, which is only likely to arise during the first year of the project or is it likely to be more endemic? For example, design and build risks are one-off, but those in the operational phase may be on-going.
- How might the risk occur and with what severity on the project? Is it likely to impact on cost, time and quality or combinations of these three factors?
- Is the risk in question independent of other risks? Care should be taken to avoid double counting.
- What is the likelihood of the risk occurring? Is there any empirical evidence to support probability assumptions?
- What distribution curve should be used to represent the risk?
- What method should be used to assess quantifiable risk? The method and all underlying assumptions should be recorded clearly.
- Having identified the risks, how might they be mitigated?

The possible strategies include piloting, adopting modular or incremental approaches, market research to improve information about the risks, flexible design solutions, more effective monitoring, and optimal allocation of roles and responsibilities.

Risk analysis should be approached seriously. Not only does it have a direct bearing on the economic case, it also has implications for the accounting treatment of the project, the contract and the post-implementation phase of the project. As such it should not be viewed as a one-off activity. The risk register should be continuously updated throughout the project. As noted in Smith (1999) from Liverpool Women's Hospital Trust's experience:

> Despite the best risk planning there are likely to be events during the course of the contract which are unforeseen. It is at these times that the benefit of proper risk planning comes into play. If foreseeable risks are planned for in the contract at an early stage, more effort and energy is available later to manage those events that are truly unforeseeable (p. 177).

Concluding remarks

The key points from this chapter may be summarised as follows.

- Be aware of the strengths and limitations of the different appraisal methods
- Economics-based methods are safer and more robust than accounting approaches. NPV is the clear favourite.
- Ensure the right cash flows are included in the NPV analysis.
- Costs and benefits already incurred (sunk costs) should be excluded.
- The recommended TDR is 6% real.
- Ensure the real TDR is applied to cash flows which are themselves expressed in real terms.
- Ensure options are appraised over the relevant time horizon. Equivalent annual costs should be computed if the options have different life spans.
- Ensure that the bases of all cash flows, including supporting assumptions, are clearly recorded.
- Sensitivity analysis should be performed on all cash flows or values which are uncertain.
- Ensure that risks are identified, evaluated and supported by robust mitigation strategies and factored into the PSC at OBC stage.
- A theoretically valid investment appraisal method on its own is no good. The data that drives the model is just as important – garbage in garbage out!

CHAPTER NINE

Tips on managing the procurement process

A business case, if approved, will invariably result in a procurement and the award of a contract to the chosen service provider(s). This chapter provides an overview of the procurement process from OJEC advertisement to contract award, and offers practical tips for managing the process to produce better and speedier procurements. Other framework procurement arrangements such as GCAT and SCAT are also summarised.

The procurement cycle

As indicated in Chapter 2, the procurement cycle is characterised by three distinct phases, each of which is informed by the business case process:

- **Phase 1:** Planning and preparing to meet the business need.
- **Phase 2:** Purchasing the solution.
- **Phase 3:** Performing the contract.

We will briefly recap the main milestones associated with these three phases before outlining the procurement process. Figure 2.2 (p. 41) presents a model of the process – the model assumes a PFI procurement. However, most of the steps and processes are generic.

Planning and preparation

By the end of this stage, the following milestones will have been established:

- production of a project initiation document
- appointment of the project team and advisers

- clear definition of the objectives and scope of the project
- clear definition of the business need in terms of outputs and outcomes
- identification of the preferred option
- development of a PSC
- completion of market sounding activities
- production of the procurement strategy and timetable
- clear position on the desired partnership, risk allocation, payment mechanism, performance regime and other commercial issues
- development of OJEC notice
- approval of the OBC
- completion of all necessary consultations, including statutory requirements such as planning permission in the case of building proposals
- development of full OBS, pre-qualification questionnaires, evaluation criteria and tender evaluation model.

As indicated in Chapter 2, much of this work will have been undertaken as part of the production of the SOC and OBC. The main exception is development of full OBS, pre-qualification questionnaires, evaluation criteria and tender evaluation model. These documents can be prepared in parallel with the approval of the OBC. The amount of work done during the planning and preparation phase will have a significant bearing on the length of the procurement process.

Purchasing the solution

The procurement is triggered by approval of the OBC. This phase is characterised by the following procurement activities:

- issue OJEC notice
- pre-qualification of bidders
- selection of the short list
- invitation to negotiate contract schedules and terms
- receipt and evaluation of bids (best and final offers (BAFO))
- produce FBC
- selection of preferred bidder and the final evaluation
- contract award and financial close.

Before contract award and financial close, a FBC should be produced to document the results of the procurement process and the selection of the preferred bidder (including reserve bidder, if this route is chosen). The FBC must demonstrate the proposed deal satisfies:

- the service requirements as specified in the OBS
- the VFM and affordability requirement
- the standard contract terms developed by the Treasury Task Force
- other approval requirements laid down by the sponsor's management board, HM Treasury and other relevant approval bodies (*see* Chapter 10 for more details).

Performing the contract

This stage comprises the following activities:

- implement the contract
- contract management
- post-implementation monitoring and evaluation.

Managing the procurement process

Clearly, there are a number of complex activities to be co-ordinated to deliver a successful, VFM procurement. Risks to the procurement time-table can be mitigated by good preparation and awareness of the procurement process.

The procuring organisation needs to have a good working knowledge of the relevant procurement regulations (or have access to advice from procurement lawyers), the likely time-scale and costs of the procurement, and the role which internal and external advisers should play in the process. The procuring body should note that even the appointment of advisers may fall within the orbit of the procurement regulations. This should be taken into account when assessing the time-scale and cost of the procurement. The risk of legal challenge from aggrieved bidders who may have incurred substantial tendering costs should always be borne in mind.

Organisations which are undertaking projects, whether PFI or conventional funding, must conform to all relevant procurement rules and regulations. They should also conduct a proper audit of the process they have followed.

Awareness of procurement regulations

The relevant UK procurement regulations which apply to PFI schemes are:

- Public Works Contracts Regulations 1991 (SI 1991/2680)
- Public Services Contracts Regulations 1993 (SI 1993/3228)
- Public Supply Contracts Regulations 1995 (SI 1995/201).

These regulations enact EC directives under UK law. The regulations apply to contracts with a value over the following thresholds:

- Public Works £3,611,395
- Public Services £93,896
- Public Supply £93,896.

These thresholds have been in place since 1 January 2000. They are updated every two years. Note, the Public Supply Contracts Regulations 1995 distinguishes between 'central government bodies' and 'other public sector contracting authorities'. For the latter, the relevant thresholds for Public Services contracts and Public Supply contracts are £144,456.

It is obligatory to advertise contracts above these thresholds in the OJEC. Otherwise, requirements may be advertised in *Government Opportunities* and/or *Contrax Weekly*, other trade periodicals, national and local newspapers as the purchaser deems necessary.

Contracts may be awarded under any of three procedures – open, restricted and negotiated. Under the 'open procedure' there is no pre-qualification stage and any number of contractors can respond to the OJEC notice. Under the 'restricted procedure' the client can confine discussions to a sample of those suppliers who have responded to the OJEC notice. However, such discussions are limited to issues of clarification rather than meaningful negotiation. Under the 'negotiated procedure', however, both of these drawbacks are avoided. The client is allowed to pre-qualify bidders and conduct detailed negotiations with those who satisfy the project requirements.

The negotiated procedure is the recommended route for PFI projects. Clients should note, however, that they do not have an automatic right to use this procedure. A justification should be provided for using the negotiated procedure.

Overview of the procurement process

Once the OBC has been approved and the preparatory work described in the previous section has been completed, formal procurement can begin. The Treasury Task Force guidance, *Step by Step Guide to the PFI Process* (1997), identifies 14 stages in the PFI procurement process. These stages also apply to conventionally financed projects. The main features of what the authors see as the key stages are summarised below. No attempt is made to reiterate the details in the Treasury Task Force's model.

Publish contract notice in OJEC

Transparency and fairness are key features of the EC procurement regulations. Public sector bodies are, therefore, required to publicise the contract notice in the OJEC. If advertisements are placed in other media (e.g. specialist press), these should not appear before the OJEC version has been despatched and should not contain any additional information to what is in the OJEC. The required format of the contract notice is described in the relevant directive.

The advertisement should contain all the necessary information about the project to enable bidders to respond appropriately to the public sector client's requirements. The type of service solutions which are acceptable should be indicated in the OJEC. This will typically include PFI, other outsourcing arrangements and capital purchase. Given the prevalence of PFI/PPP in the UK over the past decade for public sector procurements, we will focus on PFI/PPP solutions.

The OJEC should also indicate whether 'variant bids' are acceptable. The criteria that will be used to evaluate potential bidders' commercial standing and technical capacity should be stated. The advertisement should also state which procurement procedure will be used to take the project forward. The negotiated procedure with a call for competition will be generally used for PFI procurements, as it provides flexibility to the client. Guidance on how to draft an OJEC advertisement may be found in *How to Follow EC Procurement Procedure and Advertise in the OJEC*, published by HM Treasury Task Force (1998).

Under the negotiated procedure route, interested bidders are allowed at least 37 days to indicate an interest in undertaking the work. They may be expected to request a pre-qualification questionnaire and an outline specification of the project. They may also wish to visit the procuring authority's premises. These requests should be anticipated.

Pre-qualification of bidders

All parties who express an interest in the project should be sent an 'Information Memorandum' and a pre-qualification questionnaire. These should be designed to elicit information for judging whether potential bidders are technically and financially capable of satisfying the requirements of the project.

The respondents to the OJEC who have notified their interest on receipt of these documents and who have submitted the required information should be reduced to a manageable short list or long list, based on suitable and credible criteria. Regulation 14 of the procurement laws provide some of the grounds for preliminary elimination of bidders or consortium members. Bidders who have criminal convictions relating to the conduct of their business, bankruptcy, failure to pay social security contributions, etc., are automatically disqualified.

The information that should be taken into account in assessing bidders' commercial and technical standing is set out in the relevant procurement regulation. Supplementary information may be requested under the circumstances specified in Regulation 17. Factors relating to the award of the contract itself (e.g. any innovation proposed by the bidder) should not be taken into account at this stage. Such factors should be considered at the Invitation to Negotiate (ITN) stage just as factors relating to the commercial and technical standing of the bidders should not normally be considered at the ITN stage. The sifting process should be open, fair and transparent.

The grounds for eliminating a bidder from participation in the procurement process are set out in Regulation 14 of the relevant procurement regulations.

Selection of the short-list

As noted before, pre-qualification is a test of general commercial and technical suitability to meet the requirements of the project. To short-list from those who pre-qualify, suitable tests should be devised to ascertain the bidders' ability and commitment to offer an affordable, fit-for-purpose bid. These tests should consider factors such as the technical approach bidders would bring to the project, their capacity and appetite to assume risk, how they propose to finance the project and indicative price. Pricing at this stage should be approached with care since the OBS is not likely to the finalised at this stage. Pre-qualified bidders whose bids are rejected at this stage should be debriefed quickly.

The EC rejection/selection criteria and the commercial and technical information provide a sift for evaluating tenderers' potential to deliver the project. Firms with the most relevant expertise and experience are the ones who should be selected to proceed further.

Refine the project appraisal and OBS

This stage is an important precursor for issuing the ITN (or Invitation to Tender (ITT)). It is important to refine the OBC and any PSC in light of the knowledge gained from the procurement to date. In particular, the affordability of the scheme and funding commitments should be reaffirmed. This provides a sound basis to enable bidders to formulate viable bids to satisfy the project requirements.

The invitation to negotiate

The ITN provides the framework for the pre-qualified bidders to develop their detailed bids. Considerable care needs to be taken to ensure it is comprehensive, accurate and clearly drafted. Apart from enabling bidders to develop accurate proposals, it should be designed to elicit the information on which the client will need to compare bids, including comparison of private sector bids against the PSC.

The information in the ITN will need to be tailored to the requirements of the particular project. However, this is likely to address the key issues indicated in the checklist in Box 9.1.

Box 9.1: Key aspects of ITN

- Details of the project sponsors (business objectives, current con-figuration of services, activity and performance information, factors influencing demand for its services, market share, most recent income and expenditure accounts, and sources of its income, management structure, etc.)
- Details of the project (scheme objectives, functional content, list of non-clinical services to be provided under the contract, etc.)
- Output specifications for services to be provided under the con-tract and those which will be retained in-house
- Affordability
- Contract structure (summary of contractual terms governing the pro-ject, desired contract length, statement of any areas of the contract which are non-negotiable, draft project agreement and supporting schedules, etc.)
- Allocation of risks (description of allocation of risks, risk matrix reflecting the draft contract, details of any specific risks which are non-negotiable)
- Payment mechanism (structure of payment mechanism, perfor-mance monitoring regime, proposed method of indexation, market testing or benchmarking arrangements)

- Bidders' financial strategy (details of how the project will be funded, proposed shareholders, format of proposed financial model, details of assumptions underlying the financial model, etc.)
- Timetable (from submission of bids to delivery of services, statement of minimum period for which prices of fixed bids must be held prior to financial close)
- Equipment and IM&T strategy (summary of equipment and IM&T strategy, details of equipment and IM&T to be provided under the scheme, etc.)
- The PSC (description of the PSC, full risk-adjusted costs of the PSC, etc.)
- Format for bids and evaluation criteria (suggested format for bids, minimum bid requirements, confirmation that bids will be delivered within the client's affordability ceiling, summary of evaluation methodology and criteria)
- The client's position on variant and standard bids
- Tender process and timetable

Discussions with bidders during the tender period should be encouraged as this allows bidders to gain a better understanding of the client's requirements. If these discussions lead to any modification to the scope of the project, such changes should be communicated to all bidders.

The negotiating team needs to have a clear strategy before the actual negotiations begin. This should be clearly understood by each member of the team so that they all work professionally towards the same goal. This stage is likely to be very lengthy for major projects – perhaps three or four months. There is a lot of material for bidders to absorb in order to be able to formulate and prepare a formal bid.

The discussions should focus on the commercial terms of the contract and ensuring that the contracted outputs will be delivered cost-effectively. More specific objectives include:

- to ensure each bidder fully understands the public sector's service requirements;
- to ensure the public sector is clear on the solution being proposed
- to formulate an understanding by both sides to have a workable contract
- to ensure the prices are robust and any proposed solution is bankable
- to ensure the responsibilities of both parties are clearly understood and reflected in the documentation developed

- to satisfy all PFI policy requirements (optimal risk allocation, contract structure test, etc.)
- to identify and resolve all potentially contentious issues (e.g. limits of liability)
- to identify the best VFM bid (taking into account quality, achievability, realism and affordability).

To facilitate effective negotiation, the public sector client should:

- prioritise its objectives (what do we want the most from the deal?)
- anticipate the private sector's objectives (what do they want from the deal?)
- identify what they are willing to concede (i.e. things that are of relatively low value)
- identify show-stoppers
- communicate its expectations clearly
- monitor the temperature of the discussions, body language and look out for signals of movement
- anticipate when best to attempt a point of decision.

Receipt of bids

Different bidders will offer different solutions to the client's requirements. It is therefore important for these solutions to be evaluated fairly and objectively. Bidders will have already been informed of the evaluation criteria at earlier stages in the process, particularly the ITN stage.

If the client proposes to award the contract on the basis of economic advantage, this should be based on the factors in the relevant procurement Regulations. Regulation 20 of the Public Works Contracts Regulations 1991 lists these as price, period for completion, running costs, profitability and technical merit. For services (*see* Regulation 21 of the Public Services Contracts Regulations 1993), they include period for completion or delivery, quality, aesthetic and functional characteristics, technical merit, after-sales service, technical assistance and price.

Other evaluation criteria may be added to the list if they are relevant to the performance of the contract and to assessing best VFM. Factors to consider include:

- design solution and services
- affordability
- capital costs
- risk allocation

- value for money
- payment mechanism
- term of contract
- guarantees
- contingency planning
- flexibilities and options
- non-financial factors.

Evaluation of bids

The evaluation of the bids is usually undertaken by the team that has undertaken the negotiations. It is important to ensure that legal, financial and technical advisers contribute to this crucial stage. It is good practice to discuss the evaluation model with all short-listed bidders before it is finalised.

The model is likely to include factors such as financial assessment (NPV of each bidder's solution), commercial issues (acceptance of any risk transferred, deliverability of planned savings, risk management capability, etc.) and quality issues (achievability of the solution proposed, cultural fit, etc.).

Sensitivity analysis should be performed to demonstrate the impact of changes in key variables on the NPV or any weighted scores produced for each bid. The evaluation model needs to be robust and credible.

Selection of the preferred bidder

This is a crucial stage in the procurement process. The requirement in the health sector is for the terms of the contract to be developed to an advanced stage with two short-listed bidders before a preferred bidder is selected. It will require considerable resources and time to undertake two sets of negotiations simultaneously. The client will need to balance the costs to both itself and the private sector of conducting two sets of negotiations and the benefits which result from maintaining competition for longer.

Before selecting the preferred bidder the client should satisfy itself that the PFI proposal is affordable and passes the VFM test. This will require a robust and up-to-date PSC. However, the revision of the PSC should not mimic any design, engineering or operational attributes offered by the private sector.

The client should also ensure that the private sector's PFI solution is bankable and that financiers are appropriately involved. Financiers should be appointed carefully. The terms on which they provide funding will have a major bearing on the cost of the PFI solution, hence the VFM test. Factors to consider in selection of financiers include:

- experience of PFI requirements and funding projects in the sector in question
- knowledge of the sector
- acceptance of the organisation's proposed contract terms and risk allocation
- nature and duration of their due diligence strategy
- resources (including advisers) available to financiers in conducting due diligence activities on the scheme and any other schemes they may be funding.

It is recommended that the client meet each short-listed bidder's proposed financiers (funders and third-party equity providers) before selecting the two short-listed bidders. By this stage financiers should provide written support and draft term sheets to confirm their support for the scheme. In particular, they should confirm acceptance of all key contract terms, the payment mechanism, performance regime, financial model and the risks allocated to the consortium.

Before providing this commitment, financiers, in turn, will need to begin their due diligence work and satisfy themselves on all of the fundamental aspects of the transaction. Typically, the due diligence work covers issues such as:

- the quality of the procuring organisation's management team
- the way the procuring organisation is funded and its financial stability
- the business and purchasing strategy of the organisations involved in the transaction
- the risks inherent in the project, their allocation and the capabilities of the parties to manage the risks allocated to them.

The preferred bidder

Following submission of fully developed bids, the preferred bidder should be chosen from the remaining two bidders. Before selecting the preferred bidder, the short-listed bidders should have:

- agreed all key contract terms (including agreement from financiers)
- developed a full financial model

- confirmed with financiers draft term sheets for funding the project (including their confirmation of their acceptance of all key contract terms, financial model payment mechanism, and proposed risk allocation)
- submitted their best and final offers.

Before choosing the preferred bidder, it is important to ensure:

- there is agreement on the required services, outputs and outcomes over the life of the contract
- the bidder has the skills and resources to deliver the agreed services, outputs and outcomes
- there is confirmation of the allocation and management of the project risks
- the proposed bid is the most advantageous solution economically (best VFM bid when compared with the public sector comparator and other competing bids from the tendering process)
- the preferred bid is affordable and is supported by a robust and audited financial model
- there is certainty that all material commercial and contractual clauses are agreed and documented in the contract
- confirmation of the accounting treatment and financial arrangements for implementing the project.

Competition should be maintained for as long as possible. When the preferred bidder has been chosen, it is good practice to retain the remaining bidder as a 'reserve'. The reserve bidder may re-enter the negotiations if an acceptable deal cannot be reached with the preferred bidder. Having a reserve bidder in place makes the process more competitive.

To date the IM&T sector has generally adopted the practice of negotiating draft contracts and seeking best and final offers from all short-listed bidders rather than following the preferred bidder route. This approach suffers from major drawbacks. In general, it is more costly in terms of both time and transaction costs. The procuring organisation may also end up with a single bidder by default rather than by design.

Contract award and financial close

If the correct procedures have been used to select the preferred and reserve bidders, the process to contract award and financial close should be straightforward. By this stage, the preferred bidder, its subcontractors and financiers will have accepted the key commercial terms of the deal and the terms of the project documentation. The members of the consortium will have agreed to the risks allocated to them by accepting the heads of terms for the subcontractors and the financing agreements. Financiers will have completed initial due diligence.

In short, there should be few (if any) commercial issues of substance to be addressed after the preferred bidder is selected. However, considerable work will still remain at this stage, particularly the drafting of contract schedules, financing and other documentation. Ambiguities and omissions of relevant clauses should be avoided in the drafting, as these are frequently the source of disputes and claims.

Before the contract is awarded, a FBC summarising all material aspects of the deal should be submitted to the relevant approval bodies. The key requirements and content of the FBC are discussed in Chapter 6. Once the scheme has been approved, immediately before financial close, the procuring authority or public sector client will undertake a further review of the project to ensure it still satisfies the conditions on which it was approved. In line with the government's policy on openness, the public sector client will be required to publish an addendum to the FBC within one month of financial close. Once the contract has been awarded, the client is required to place a contract award notice in the OJEC within 48 days of awarding the contract.

Contract management

This is a distinct phase that follows on from the procurement process. The requirements for contract management have been addressed in Chapter 7.

Suffice to recap, the client will need to put mechanisms in place to ensure the facility is completed on time and to the required standard. It will also need to ensure that the level of services delivered over the life span of the contract fully meets the standards laid down in the OBS and the relevant contract documentation. The client will need to appoint someone with the appropriate expertise to monitor compliance with the contract during the various phases of the project.

Time-scales

The time-scale for completing the whole process will depend on a number of factors, most notably the procurement route, the size and type of project, the complexity of the project and the dedication of the project team. In the case of procurement of a major hospital scheme, the whole time-scale can

Table 9.1: Milestones and indicative timetable for IM&T and major capital projects using the negotiated route

Milestone	IM&T projects – duration (days)	Major capital projects – duration (days)
OJEC notice	1	1
Deadline for expressions of interest	37	37
Deadline for pre-qualification	14	28
Evaluation of pre-qualification submissions and long list of up to six	14	21
Deadline for response to preliminary ITN	42	60
Evaluation of response and short list of three	21	28
Deadline for fully priced bids to preliminary ITN	49	60
Evaluation down to two	optional	21
Negotiations with two or three (depending on route chosen)	42	56
Issue ITT (deadline for fixed price bids)	21	28
Evaluation down to one	14	21
Negotiations leading up to FBC submission	21	77
FBC approval	normally undertaken in parallel with supplier negotiations for IM&T projects	90
Financial close, due diligence and contract award	28*	30
Total	304**	558***

* IM&T projects to date are generally not funded from third-party finance
** approx 10 months
*** approx 18 months

be expected to last 18 months on average. For major IM&T projects, the process can be completed within 12 months (*see* Table 9.1).

Managing procurement risks

- the length of the procurement process and the quality of the deal which emerges from it will critically depend on:
- the degree of preparation of the procuring organisation(s)
- the calibre and experience of the project team (including the negotiating team)

- the size and complexity of the project
- the number of stakeholders involved
- the level of approval required
- the number of responses to the pre-qualification questionnaire
- The approach to risk identification and project management.

As noted in Chapter 2, the SOC and OBC processes should be seen as an integral part of the preparation for the procurement. It is during this stage (i.e. the OBC phase) that the full procurement strategy is developed. The procurement options at this stage include the traditional OJEC route and call-off arrangements from existing framework contracts. In the case of IM&T procurements, the latter includes the various Catalogue arrangements which are operated by the Buying Agency, OGC. Other procurement options are likely to become available as digital technology develops.

Perhaps the best-known of these Catalogues are G-CAT and S-CAT, both of which are compliant with the EU procurement regulations. G-CAT provides a ready-made framework contract to help departments and agencies procure IT products and services speedily and cost-effectively. A recent, NAO report, *Modernising Procurement*, found that G-CAT has a major effect in reducing procurement costs. A major source of these savings results from bulk purchase and improved pricing from supplier competitions. Further details are available on-line at www.gcat.co.uk and www.scat.co.uk.

The procurement environment is also likely to change in future as e-procurement gathers pace. The comprehensive review study, *Efficiency in Civil Government Procurement*, identified a number of areas where e-commerce should be introduced to expedite and enhance the procurement process. Peter Gershon (now Permanent Secretary of the OGC) elaborated on this in his review of commerce within the public sector. A new organisation, OGC, has been established to implement the various recommendations, including those which focus on the requirements for e-commerce.

Once e-procurement is properly airborne, the benefits are likely to be colossal. The following benefits are anticipated:

- Improved interface between suppliers and government departments and agencies, leading to time savings and reduced costs for all the parties.
- Reduced paper trail in tendering exercises, thus saving costs and improving the audit of the procurement process.
- Speedier procurements arising from electronic tendering and reduced bureacracy.
- Increased visibility and accessibility of government procurement.
- Improved savings on low-value transactions. For example, case study evidence indicates a reduction in processing costs from £60 to £10 an order.

Concluding remarks

This chapter has outlined the main stages involved in a PFI procurement. While it is no substitute for first-hand experience of the process itself, it should nevertheless alert procurers to what to expect and how best to prepare for the procurement. In addition, it is recommended that they consult other relevant public sector bodies about their experience of undertaking PFI procurements.

The following key points deserve special emphasis.

- Good, all-round preparation is crucial to securing the desired outcome from the procurement process, regardless of the method of procurement.
- A balanced and experienced project team should be established from the outset to advise on all aspects of the procurement. Invariably, this should include legal, financial and relevant technical skills.
- The procurement should not begin until the relevant approvals have been secured (usually the OBC).
- Each of the 14 stages in the procurement process should be properly understood.
- Be clear about the procurement rules and procurement routes and ensure these are followed in spirit and letter.
- Take steps to streamline the procurement process and produce high-quality documentation to reduce time-scales and transaction costs.
- Avoid choosing the preferred bidder prematurely.
- Remember that competition is ultimately the best guarantor of VFM.

CHAPTER TEN

Producing and submitting the business case

This chapter reviews some of the 'process issues' that arise from producing and submitting the business case for approval. It summarises approval thresholds, information sources for populating business cases, associated time-scales, the standard approval criteria and key 'gateway review' checkpoints.

The role of planning

It should be clear by now that producing a fit-for-purpose business case for an investment proposal requires careful planning and professional input from a wide range of personnel.

From the outset, a project plan or project initiation document should be produced to identify the inputs required – both personnel and financial resources. Allowance should be made for inputs from senior managers, the organisation's board, staff time and external resources. Identification of personnel on its own is not sufficient. Roles and responsibilities need to be clearly defined. A Senior Responsible Officer should be appointed to take overall responsibility for delivering the project.

The amount of staff and financial resources required will depend on the type and size of the case. Lessons from the experience of public and private sector organisations suggest that, as a broad rule of thumb, a budget of 1% of the capital value of the investment should be set aside to prepare the business case.

A suitably comprised team should be established to produce and quality assure the business case. This should recognise that input will be required from different specialists who understand both the technical and service requirements of the project. The 'five-case model' provides a general guide to the type of skills required to produce the various components of the case. They must reflect the nature of the investment.

Typically, the following generic skills are required:

- Strategic case – business and strategic planning skills.
- Economic case – investment appraisal skills (ability to define objectives clearly, identify options, cost and evaluate options, undertake risk analysis), 'subject specialists' (e.g. for construction of hospitals, input is needed from architects, engineers, surveyors, planners, estate managers, etc.).
- Commercial case – commercial law, contracts, corporate finance.
- Financial case – financial analysis, costing and general accounting.
- Project management case – project managers.

The importance of consultation

The project plan must allow for meaningful engagement and consultation with those who will be affected by the investment proposal and who will be involved in the approval process. The stakeholders will typically span a number of external organisations as well as the organisation's own staff.

The way consultation is handled will have a major bearing on the success or otherwise of the proposal. If stakeholders are consulted from the outset and throughout the process of developing the business case, this increases the likelihood of securing commitment and 'buy-in' to the proposed investment.

Stakeholders can add a great deal of value to the decision-making process. These include helping to:

- refine the objectives of the project to ensure they are 'SMART'
- scope the project
- identify options (including the preferred solution)
- identify costs, benefits and risks
- implement the preferred option
- realise benefits
- fund the project in some cases (e.g. investments in the NHS are generally initiated by NHS trusts but funded by health authorities and other commissioners of their services).

Time-scale

The time-scale for producing a SOC, OBC and FBC will depend on a number of factors, most notably availability of requisite skills the nature of the investment, complexity, novelty, amount of resources allocated to complete the various tasks, number of stakeholders involved in the consultation and approval process, and frequency and flexibility of meetings to sign off the various outputs. Small, routine investments may take a few months but larger and less straight-forward projects will take considerably longer.

For most investments in the public sector, a broad guide is:

- production of SOC – up to three months
- production of OBC – two to six months (depending on the amount of work done at the SOC stage and the complexity of the project)
- production of FBC – three to six months (note, some of the work required to produce the FBC can be done in parallel with conducting the tendering exercise, but the FBC cannot be completed until the parameters of the proposed deal have been agreed). The time-scale should also make allowance for other activities associated with the business case and procurement process (*see* Chapter 9, particularly section on procurement process). These include the review and approval process, production of other documents to support the procurement process (e.g. OBS, evaluation methodology, pre-qualification documents, ITN documents, etc.).

Information requirements and sources

In Chapter 2, we outlined the issues which should be addressed in a SOC, OBC and FBC. The information required to address these issues will come from a variety of primary and secondary sources. This is likely to include management information from past investments undertaken by the organisation or from similar projects from other organisations, results of relevant post-project evaluation studies, policy documents, the organisation's business and corporate plans, interviews and tailor-made workshops.

We have found from our experience that the workshop approach is particularly effective in generating quality information to populate the case. At the same time, it provides a medium for stakeholders to participate meaningfully in developing the project.

We recommend a minimum of five one-day workshops with direct participation from the key stakeholders, both internal and external. It is important for the former to include directors, other senior managers and users.

The proposed workshops are shown in Table 10.1, together with objectives, key participants and deliverables. Other workshops may be devised as appropriate. The workshops proposed are designed to illustrate the value of this means of eliciting information to populate the business case.

Table 10.1: Proposed workshops

Workshops	Objectives	Key participants	Output(s)
Workshop 1: scope and options generations	• To define and agree needs, scope and investment objectives • To agree desired service outputs and outcomes • To define and agree benefit criteria for assessing the options • To identify options for meeting the investment objectives	Board members, project manager, user representatives, relevant external stakeholders, financial adviser, facilitator	• SMART investment objectives • List of benefit criteria • Long list of options • Fundamentals of the SOC
Workshop 2: assessment of options	• To sift the long-listed options and generate a short-list • To identify and assess costs, benefits and risks associated with short-listed options (including type, timing, value)	Director of finance, economic adviser, user representatives, external stakeholders, project manager, facilitator	• Short-listed options with preliminary assessments • Outline benefit realisation plan
Workshop 3: development of 'reference project' or public sector comparator (including risk apportionment)	• To develop the PSC and address all relevant issues, including risks, affordability and implementation	Director of finance, economic adviser, user representatives, external stakeholders, project manager, facilitator	• Preliminary PSC with indicative costings • Fundamentals of the economic and financial cases
Workshop 4: service requirements, payment mechanism and contractual issues	• To develop a risk allocation matrix (RAM) • To identify and agree payment mechanisms • To identify parameters for the desired deal with service provider(s)	Director of finance, economic adviser, legal adviser, user representatives, external stakeholders, project manager, facilitator	• Preliminary RAM • Desired payment mechanism • Agreed position on key contractual issues • Fundamentals of the commercial case
Workshop 5: procurement strategy, process and project management	• To identify and agree the procurement strategy for the project • To develop the project plan (including project team, resources and timetable)	Director of finance, economic adviser, user representatives, external stakeholders, project manager, facilitator	• Procurement strategy • Project plan • Fundamentals of the project management case

Presenting the business case

The needs of those who have authority to approve the project should be considered from the outset. Three key questions to consider are:

- Who needs to approve the project?
- What criteria will they apply in considering whether or not to approve the project?
- What information do I need to submit in the business case to demonstrate compliance with the stipulated criteria? These vary from government department to department, both from within and without (HM Treasury delegations).

Approval thresholds

For NHS-initiated investments, depending on the nature and size of the project, the typical decision makers are the organisation's chief executive, board, its main commissioner(s), Regional Office, NHS Executive and HM Treasury.

The current delegated limits for NHS organisations are shown in Table 10.2. If a scheme is judged to be novel or contentious, approval will be required from HM Treasury regardless of its capital value. This rule holds fast for all public sector organisations.

Approval criteria

Departments regularly review their approval criteria. The prevailing criteria are normally published. For illustrative purposes, we reproduce below the criteria we have helped to develop to appraise NHS IM&T projects. Note, these are mapped onto the 'five-case model'. Although the details of these criteria are likely to change, we would expect the substance to remain intact. Criteria such as value for money and affordability tests will always remain pertinent.

Assessing the validity of the strategic case

1.1   Is there an organisational overview, setting out details of the organisation, its structure, its financial position, services provided, population and commissioners served?

Table 10.2: Approval thresholds for NHS organisations (2001)

Total capital cost	Approval authority
Greater than £0.25m for NHS trusts with turnover under £30m per year	OBC and FBC to Regional Office
Greater than £0.6m for NHS trusts with turnover between £30m and £80m per year	OBC and FBC to Regional Office
Greater than £1m	OBC and FBC to Regional Office for approval. FBC to NHS Executive for 'sampling' (if selected, approval is required from NHS Executive)
Greater than £4m	OBC and FBC to Regional Office for approval. FBC to NHS Executive for 'sampling' (if selected, approval is required from NHS Executive and HM Treasury)
Greater than £10m	OBC to Regional Office for approval. Approval of FBC is required from both Regional Office and HM Treasury
Greater than £50m	OBC to Regional Office for approval. Approval of FBC is required from Regional Office, HM Treasury and relevant Ministers
NHS IM&T projects: Less than £20m whole-life costs	OBC and FBC to Regional Office for approval (check whether Regional Office in question has been 'accredited'). If not accredited, submit OBC and FBC to NHS Executive Headquarters for approval as well
Greater than £20m whole-life costs	FBC requires approval by Regional Office, NHS Executive and HM Treasury

1.2 Is there a summary of the organisation's current IM&T capability, including, for example, the configuration of current systems, the existing level of integration, the extent of paper-based systems, the level of IM&T (information processing) expertise? How does this IM&T provision compare with that of other similar organisations?

1.3 Is the 'gap' in IM&T provision, supporting health service delivery, identified?

1.4 Is a summary or copy of the organisation's IM&T strategy part of the business case, and does this and the case demonstrate:

- that the strategy is consistent with the local implemenation strategy?
- that the strategy itself is an integral part of the business strategy and is reflected in the corporate mission statement and the local Health Improvement Programme?
- that the strategy will meet the likely future demand on IM&T support of health service delivery, taking account of general NHS trends, the strategic direction of the trust and wider NHS (including proposed development of specialised services), and support from commissioners (including GPs and other local stakeholders as appropriate)?
- that the strategy includes an indication of the expected cost savings (and cost avoidance) and indicative costs for meeting each of the IM&T provisions set out in the strategy?
- that the strategic context includes a statement of the organisation's approach to PFI in IM&T provision (scope for involving the private sector, desired risk allocation, possible risk transfer mechanisms, etc.)?
- that the proposed IT procurement is part of the organisation's IM&T strategy?
- that the procurement is in line with the NHS Executive's national information strategy and conforms to national communications and other standards? Cross-references to local implementation strategies may be helpful here.

1.5 For new-build schemes, has proper account been taken of how best IM&T services should be procured? Have interdependencies been identified?

At FBC stage

1.6 Have the earlier demand assumptions in support of the size and scope of the investment been reassessed since the OBC and confirmed as still valid?

1.7 Has the IM&T strategy been updated since the OBC and are the original objectives for the procurement still valid?

1.8 Is there a clear statement of the objectives of the IM&T investment? Is it clear what health service needs are being pursued through the investment?

1.9 Are these objectives directly linked to the organisation's health service and business objectives as embodied in the IM&T strategy?

1.10 Are the objectives SMART?

Assessing the validity of the economic case

2.1 Has consideration been given to a sufficiently wide range of options (including a 'do nothing' or 'do minimum' option) for meeting the project objectives?

2.2 Do the do nothing/do minimum options demonstrate that due account has been taken of achieving the same benefits from better use of existing assets?

2.3 Are options described in output and functional terms without specifying the solution in technical or method terms?

2.4 Are sound reasons provided for including or excluding each option?

2.5 Are the criteria for short-listing options clear and consistent with existing guidance?

2.6 Have the short-listed options been adequately described to facilitate assessment of costs, benefits and risks?

2.7 Have all **relevant** capital and running costs been identified and properly assessed?

2.8 Do the IM&T investment objectives lead to a set of five to ten high-level (measurable) criteria, the benefits criteria, by which the progress and success of this investment can be ascertained? Is the baseline situation adequately specified?

2.9 Has a comparative appraisal of benefits been undertaken and tabulated? In particular, is it clear who (or what operational area or department or unit) has responsibility for realising each benefit?

2.10 Have costs and benefits been assessed from the perspective of the public sector?

2.11 Have 'sunk costs', transfer payments and other non-resource costs been excluded from the economic appraisal?

2.12 Have the relevant costs/benefits been adequately identified and described to facilitate assessment?

2.13 Have all relevant cash-releasing and non-cash-releasing benefits been properly and realistically assessed?

2.14   Have all non-quantifiable benefits been properly assessed (e.g. by weighting and scoring techniques)?

2.15   Have costs and benefits been stated in constant prices? Is the base year clearly specified?

2.16   Have costs and benefits been discounted at the right discount rate (currently 6%)?

2.17   Have all the important assumptions underlying all cash-flow/NPV calculations been stated?

2.18   Is there any evidence of double counting of costs and benefits?

2.19   Have the risks associated with the preferred option been appropriately costed? Is there a description of the methodology used to quantify and value risks? (At OBC stage, the work should be kept to a minimum. Broad rules of thumb may be used to establish a suitable allowance for risks. A full analysis, based on 'expected values', is required at FBC stage. Sensitivity analysis should also be conducted on the key assumptions underlying the risk analysis, with risks themselves categorised into 'high', 'medium' and 'low'.)

2.20   Are the values of the risks clearly explained and the assumptions underlying the nature, timing and potential impact of the risks set out?

2.21   Has sufficient sensitivity analysis (including 'switching values') been undertaken on key assumptions and variables with uncertain values?

2.22   Where supporting evidence is provided in an appendix, is this consistent with the results presented in the main body of the text and with other option evaluation analyses?

2.23   Is there a clear recommendation of a preferred option?

2.24   Are the reasons for selecting the preferred option clearly stated?

2.25   Is there any evidence to suggest that the preferred option was not selected on the basis of the appraisal process (e.g. proper consideration of relative costs and benefits of short-listed options, risks and uncertainties)?

At FBC stage

2.26   Is there a summary of the OBC, including a description of the long- and short-listed options considered, results of the economic appraisal, benefits appraisal, financial analysis and sensitivity analysis? Where there have been changes in the underlying assumptions since the OBC, does the FBC demonstrate how the changes have affected the ranking of options, including benefits?

2.27   Is there evidence that the objectives of the IM&T investment are still valid, and that the proposed solution will meet these objectives?

2.28   Have the results of the economic appraisal from the OBC stage been revised and updated?

2.29   Is there a valid and up-to-date PSC for evaluating VFM? Is this the best conventionally financed option(s) offered during the procurement process?

2.30   Is there a clear recommendation of the preferred option from the procurement? Are the reasons for the preferred option clearly stated?

2.31   Does the preferred option from the tendering process conclusively satisfy the VFM (including risk transfer in the case of PFI solutions) test?

2.32   Is there a clear statement of additional benefits attainable from any higher-cost option offered during the procurement process?

2.33   Does the appraisal identify and clearly define all the major risks and uncertainties associated with the short-listed options and the preferred option in particular?

2.34   Has the high-level assessment and valuation of benefits in the OBC been substantially developed for the preferred option in the FBC? Is commitment to benefits realisation more strongly demonstrated?

Assessing the validity of the commercial case

3.1   Has private finance been considered as a procurement method? And has the procurement method (public or private funding) been chosen on clear and demonstrable value for money grounds? Where appropriate, has the scope of any PFI scheme been informed by market sounding?

3.2   Does the case demonstrate understanding of the objectives and requirements for PFI? Is this understanding reflected in the RAM and risk transfer mechanisms?

3.3   Has account been taken of potential private sector risks (e.g. bankruptcy of service provider)?

3.4   Does the timetable meet all applicable requirements of EC public procurement directives?

3.5   Does the timetable allow sufficient time for completion of all identified procurement project tasks, such as supplier negotiations and other milestones associated with PFI?

3.6   Does the timetable identify and allow for all supporting tasks to be accomplished, such as benefits identification and planning, the required approvals process and associated organisational change management processes?

3.7   Does the draft OJEC advertisement meet legal requirements as appropriate for the proposed procurement? (*see* Annex D of HSG(95)48).

3.8   Does the case provide an outline of how the contract will be developed?

At FBC stage

3.9   Does the FBC demonstrate that the appropriate procurement procedures have been followed as set out in POISE and as required by EC directives? Is a copy of the OJEC notice included in the FBC?

3.10   Was the short-listing evaluation of supplier responses to the OJEC advertisement conducted in the appropriate manner?

3.11   Was the short-listing of proposals, in response to the OBS conducted properly?

3.12   From the description of the responses received, was a wide range of responses elicited, and did the evaluation process place due emphasis on PFI proposals?

3.13   Is there a description of the preferred service provider?

3.14   Is there a sound RAM for the preferred option indicating how the risks might be apportioned between the public and private sectors and the mechanisms for effecting risk transfer? (This should be present in outline at OBC stage.)

3.15   Are reasons presented for the proposed risk allocation?

3.16   Does the FBC provide a clear summary of the contract, including preferred contract length, proposed key contractual clauses and any personnel/TUPE issues? This should address all the key headings, explain the proposed payment mechanism and tie in to the risk analysis.

3.17   Has the Treasury Taskforce guidance been followed on the contractual provisions?

3.18   Have the risks that have been transferred to suppliers been reflected in the terms and conditions for the contract?

Assessing the validity of the financial case

4.1   Is public capital available to fund the scheme?

4.2   Has a financial appraisal been undertaken to assess the revenue and net price implications of the preferred option on commissioners? Has the financial impact of the preferred option been compared with the organisation's current expenditure on IM&T or with the 'do minimum' option?

4.3   Does this analysis take into account the cost of risk and the full whole-life costs for the investment? Does the revenue implications assessment include capital charges and other relevant costs?

4.4   Has the impact of the investment on the trust's balance sheet, cash-flow position, and income and expenditure account been assessed?

4.5   Is the methodology for the financial appraisal clearly recorded? Have all key assumptions underlying the financial appraisal been explicitly stated?

4.6   Has suitable sensitivity analysis on these assumptions been undertaken (including switching values on sensitive indicators)?

4.7   Is the project affordable? Has this been subject to suitable sensitivity analysis?

4.8   Is there flexibility to fund any additional revenue requirements or absorb any affordability gap? Is the trust capable of managing any funding shortfall? What specific proposals are put forward for managing the shortfall? Are they adequate?

4.9   Is there written support from commissioners documenting agreement with the need to invest in the preferred IM&T solution? If there is an affordability gap, do the commissioners indicate support of trust plans for covering this?

4.10 Is there evidence of the commissioner's involvement in the development of the IM&T strategy and the proposed investment in particular?

At FBC stage, the affordability analysis for the preferred option must be subject to a more detailed analysis than in the OBC.

4.11 Is there a written opinion from the director of finance and the health organisation's external auditor that assesses the balance sheet treatment of the scheme in line with current guidance?

Assessing the validity of the project management case

5.1   Has the organisational and cultural impact of the IM&T strategy been considered and are the measures in place adequate to manage change successfully? Is the identified impact consistent with wider organisational strategies, e.g. human resources, estates or clinical services? Factors to consider will include:

• complexity and size of preferred option
• amount of business process engineering needed

- technophobia
- senior management commitment
- ownership of preferred option
- review of organisational practices and procedures
- changing health service objectives, etc.

5.2   Is the nature, timing and potential impact of the risks clearly explained and are their implications understood?

5.3   Is there an adequate risk-management strategy for managing all risks that will be retained by the public sector? (At OBC stage, a broad, outline risk management strategy is sufficient.)

5.4   Is there evidence that security and confidentiality have been addressed in accordance with the Caldicott principles?

5.5   Has an adequate contract management strategy been developed?

5.6   Is there a detailed benefits realisation plan based on quantified and measurable benefits?

5.7   Is there evidence that the preferred option, including performance targets and functionality, is fully supported by users, including local health professionals, where appropriate?

5.8   Is there a commitment to assign responsibility for realising benefits to an individual, or group, with sufficient authority to deliver?

5.9   Is it clear what benefits are to be realised by which business/clinical operational departments?

5.10 Is the division of responsibilities and hand-over arrangements clear between those responsible for delivering benefits during implementation and those responsible for delivery benefits during the operational phase?

5.11 Have effective benefits realisation monitoring and reporting structures been established?

5.12 In a PFI context, is it clear what benefits are to be delivered by the NHS organisation and what benefits are the responsibility of the supplier? How will the latter be monitored?

5.13 Have cash-releasing benefits been separated from non-cash-releasing benefits? Does the case demonstrate how cash is to be released?

5.14 Is there evidence of a clear recognition that the investment on its own will not deliver the expected benefits (e.g. need for changes in working practices)? Is it clear how those changes will be brought about and managed?

5.15 Does the business case include a summary of PRINCE project management structure, including the CV of the project manager (or job description if not yet appointed), membership of project board and plans for user involvement?

5.16   Does the PRINCE project structure give assurance that the project has sufficient backing by, and commitment from, senior executives and user groups to underpin a successful project?

5.17   The chief executive should sign-off the OBC and FBC, and board support should be explicit. The chief executive will ideally sit on the project board in some capacity. Such arrangements should have been described in the project management section. Are these aspects adequately dealt with?

5.18   Is there a sufficient and adequately skilled IM&T resource to manage successfully the procurement, implementation and operational stages? Account should be taken of the total IM&T demands on IM&T resources as indicated in the IM&T strategy, and of how much the organisation is responsible for managing the IM&T service and/or the service supplier. The organisation could consider the (interim) use of other external sources if necessary. These sources must not include the supplier.

5.19   Is there a clear definition of the scope of the post-project evaluation, resources and personnel approaches to be adopted (e.g. PROBE), time-scales and specific milestones reviews? Is the emphasis correctly balanced, taking due account of benefits realisation?

5.20   Have responsibilities for evaluation been assigned, identifying named individuals where possible, and have lines of reporting been established?

Consistency with OGC gateway review criteria

These criteria are consistent with OGC's gateway review questions (*see* www.ogc.gov.uk). One notable difference, however, is that OGC allows for continuous monitoring throughout the life span of projects.

Formal reviews are recommended at five checkpoints as indicated in Table 10.3. In summary, these are at the 'SOC stage', 'OBC stage', 'FBC stage', 'contract award stage' and 'operational stage'.

Appendix 1 contains key review criteria developed recently by the authors from the following main sources:

- the NAO publication entitled 'Assessing VFM in PFI Deals'
- OGC gateway criteria (February 2001)
- department guidance on OBC and FBC reviews.

This has been tailored to the requirements of the 'five-case model' within SOCs, OBCs and FBCs and bridges a number of gaps which the authors have identified within existing guidance.

Table 10.3: Summary of OGC's gateway reviews

Gateway reviews	Key high-level issues focus on
Gateway review 1 – Business justification confirmed? The purpose of GR1 is to confirm the robustness of the initial business case (essentially a SOC), establish that the feasibility study is complete and secure authority to proceed to the next stage (i.e. 'define procurement strategy stage')	Review of current stage (robustness of underlying assumptions, etc.) Potential for success (understanding of users' needs, scope, options, etc.) Risk management (risk identification and assessment, preliminary market soundings, etc.) State of readiness for next stage (GR2) – resources, project management arrangements, consultation with stakeholders, etc.
Gateway review 2 – Procurement method and source of supply confirmed – essentially OBC stage. The purpose of GR2 is to define the project in greater detail, validate its viability and assess the readiness for 'invite, evaluate and refine tenders' phase	Same issues as GR1 but in more detail, plus an assessment of state of readiness for the 'invite, evaluate, refine tenders' phase (i.e. statement of requirements, project acceptance strategy, project plan and resources for satisfactorily completing remaining stages)
Gateway review 3 – Investment decision confirmed – essentially FBC stage. The purpose of GR3 is to confirm that the recommended contract decision is appropriate, likely to meet users needs, affordable, passes the VFM test, etc.	Same issues as GR2 but in more detail, plus an assessment of state of readiness to proceed satisfactorily to the next stage – award and implement contract (e.g. internal and external approval, long-term contract management plan, benefit realisation plan, etc.)
Gateway review 4 – Readiness for service confirmed – contract award. At the end of GR4, the contracted service 'goes live', hence this review aims to confirm state of readiness for service and reviewing the basis for evaluation of ongoing performance.	Same issues as GR3 with major focus on service needs, affordability, consultation with internal and external stakeholders, training, potential for success, and readiness for next stage – 'manage and operate contract'
Gateway review 5 – 'In service' benefits confirmed – operational phase? During this phase, periodic checks are made to ensure project is meeting users' needs within the agreed business case and contract parameters.	This phase focuses on whether users' needs are being met, performance of service provider(s), benefit realisation, contractual management, relationship with users/stakeholders, etc.

The number of criteria in each instance has been limited to the 'top 15'. Against each criterion the evidence required to demonstrate compliance is shown. A section is also included for completion by the reviewer of the business case (*see* Appendix 1).

Concluding remarks

We have now completed our exposition on the 'five-case model'. We have also provided guidance on the underpinning tools, techniques and processes.

We share the firm conviction that use of the model will lead to a major improvement in the way public sector (and, arguably, private sector) projects are designed, implemented and managed. The model offers the prospect of better decision making, improved resource allocation and win–win outcomes for government departments, the tax-paying public and suppliers. It will help to reduce the incidence of procurement failures such as the Millennium Dome, the National Insurance Recording System, Passport Office information system, Home Office's Case Recording and Management System, British Library and Channel Tunnel.

Consider, for example, the recent experience of the Home Office in procuring a Case Recording and Management System (CRAMS). In their review of this procurement, the National Audit Office (2001) found major weaknesses in the way the project was developed and implemented. Drawing on the 'five-case model', the following extracts convey the flavour of the shortcomings:

Box 10.1: Some weaknesses in the implementation of the Home Office's Case Recording and Management System

Strategic Case: Poor specification of expected outputs and outcomes; failure to identify users' needs properly and to develop effective contractual arrangements to meet those needs; poor communication between the key stakeholders (e.g. the Home Office and the local Probation Services). 'The Home Office did not ensure that the development of CRAMS kept pace in all respects with changing business needs' – p. 3.

Economic Case: Over-run of full economic cost by 70% at constant prices above the planned expenditure. 'Costs and achievements have not been monitored against projections in the original business case' – p. 3. Risks were not properly identified and appraised. 'The

Home Office underestimated the technical risks associated with trans-ferring an existing system onto the network ... the system's accept-ability and usability were unknown' – p. 4.

Commercial Case: Failure to define an effective contractual arrange-ment with the service provider: 'The enabling agreement with [the service provider] is largely open-ended, with additional expenditure commitments being made as and when required' – p. 2. No clear definition of outputs, payment mechanism, and service monitoring: '... there were unnecessary purchase orders, duplication and overlap, and a risk of over-payment ... Legal advice ... Suggests that any new pur-chase orders raised under the enabling agreement are unlawful' – p. 5.

Financial Case: No affordability problems identified, but given the open-ended nature of the agreement, there is the potential for short-term and long-term affordability pressures.

Project Management Case: Failure to form a viable and suitably skilled project team; no clear definition of roles and responsibilities; no contingency plan to deal with turnover of key managers ('in its first seven years ... the programme team had seven programme direc-tors' – p. 2); inadequate communication strategy; failure to develop a robust risk management strategy and benefit realisation plan. 'The performance of the [service provider] was not managed effectively. Monitoring of service levels against the enabling agreement was sporadic' – p. 5.

Source: National Audit Office (2001)

Readers are reminded that the model is not intended to be used as a rigid, mechanical drill. It is a flexible aid to decision making. The book will achieve its purpose if it leads project sponsors to pay greater attention to strategic fit, value for money, supply-side capabilities, affordability and strong project management capacity throughout the various stages of the capital investment process. In a nutshell, this is the essence of the 'five-case model'. It is failure to address these five core sets of issues which has led to the dissipation of hundreds of millions of pounds of public and private sector resources in recent years.

Organisations and individuals who have used the 'five-case model' have confirmed its power as a decision-making tool. We conclude with a sample of the feedback, which they have volunteered. Comments on the model and requests for training in its use should be sent to csmith@waitrose.com.

'As one of the leading firms of advisors on the development of business cases, we have found that applying the five-case model has proved to be of great benefit both in structuring the content required in a business case, and also in making the business case a key tool for improving communications between a project and its stakeholders – its great strength is its simplicity and clarity, which makes a potentially dry subject much more accessible to management and users alike.'

John Farenden
Partner in Secta Consulting Ltd

'Decisions on major investments can be very difficult to make. Within the NHS, there is a perception of failure, particularly around large IT projects, and it is therefore even more critical that appropriate judgements are made.

Making Sense of Public Sector Investments: the 'five-case model' in decision making sets out very clear guidance around the process and structure for developing business cases to support such investment decisions.

The health service is currently engaged in implementing the NHS Plan, the Government's strategy for delivering a national service of consistently high quality, designed around the needs of patients. This highlights the need for national action to co-ordinate and facilitate communication across all partners engaged in delivering healthcare. As a result, many difficult investment decisions need to be made, concerning the scope of national services, the most appropriate way of delivering those services and ways of ensuring that the anticipated benefits are achieved.

The five-case model has provided a superb tool for assisting in this process, particularly with the concentration in the Strategic Case on the business needs and investment objectives (often not clearly thought through) and the options framework, which forms the backbone of the Economic Case. The Financial Case and Commercial Case help to focus on the affordability issues as well as the procurement options and considerations. The Project Management Case provides much-needed assistance in considering the achievability of schemes. It is important to know that objectives can be achieved, benefits realised and risks managed. Both authors have been heavily involved in recent NHS projects and have provided invaluable help and assistance. This book has therefore been written 'in the heat of battle' and this is reflected in the examples used and the advice given.

It is my firm opinion that the advice within this book, if considered carefully and applied sensibly, will provide much greater clarity of thought around investment decisions. It will therefore help strengthen the case for those projects that can succeed, and help to provide early warning of those that will not.'

Jeremy Thorp
Head of Infrastructure and Standards
Information Policy Unit
Department of Health

'The five-case model is becoming the standard for presentation of business cases in Government and the wider public sector, and is equally applicable to organisations within the private sector seeking to make robust investment decisions.

In the context of staged approval/decision making (the SOC; the OBC and the FBC), it has been welcomed by both senior management who must make decisions, and by the planners, analysts, specialists and users etc. who must deliver solutions and live with them on a daily basis. Why should this be so? This book addresses various reasons. But from my personal experience, the reason is that the five-case model highlights the 'grey areas' – the problematic and difficult issues that underline investment decisions – which have been gently sidelined, or even buried under the carpet in the past. Too often the approach to a business case has been, 'How do I justify the investment?' rather than 'Is this investment justified?'.

Over the years a great deal of hair loss by the authors of the business cases has been in specifying and appraising options. Often, with a new IS/IT system, for example, there may be dozens and dozens of options, and any approving authority worth its salt can think of half a dozen additional options not considered in the business case – the outcome often being to delay the project. The approach recommended here, the Options Framework – of breaking options into component parts (business scope, technical solution, service delivery, implementation and funding, etc.) for comparison against investment objectives and critical success factors, to reach a short list for further analysis and costing – is a *powerful tool*. It provides a systematic and sequential approach to covering a comprehensive and wide range of options in a meaningful and objective way.

The text provides an invaluable starting point for its intended audience. However, I would emphasise the importance of stakeholder analysis in the advent of pandepartmental, cross-cutting projects in the public sector (in support of initiatives such as the Joined-Up Government Agenda and the Cabinet Office's e-Commerce Strategy). And related to this, the importance of quantifying and targeting non-financial benefits – for example, looking at the public as a stakeholder in appropriate cases.

On a cautionary note, it is noticeable that projects are looking to use the commercial case to make the procurement attractive to the private sector. Care must be taken to avoid such problems as 'cherry picking' or the bundling of disparate services without careful thought, e.g. estate management and IT services.

This book is well worth reading at the earliest stage in project planning and provides an invaluable source of up-to-date thinking and reference material in a single publication.'

RAC Dunstan
Consultant
Strategic Assignment Consultancy
OGC, HM Treasury

Review criteria

Stage: Review of the SOC
Purpose: To establish the business justification for the proposed investment.

Key review criteria	*Evidence required*
Strategic case	
1 Is the proposed project an integral part of the organisation's business strategy?	• Extracts from business and other relevant strategies • Reference to relevant government and organisational policies
2 Is the proposed investment sufficiently large and stand alone to form a project or could it be more sensibly undertaken as part of another programme or project?	• Relevant extracts from business and other strategies • Reference to scoping documentation • Relevant extracts from strategy board minutes
3 Are the investment objectives and underpinning business needs defined clearly and supported by the key stakeholders and customers?	• SMART investment objectives • Evidence of stakeholder and customer involvement and support
4 Is the scope for potential change to current services and business processes clearly defined?	• Clear statement of business outcomes and service outputs • Statement of any security and confidentiality issues
5 Have the main benefits been clearly defined by key stakeholders and customers, alongside arrangements for their realisation?	• Direct and indirect to the organisation and wider public sector Cash (£) and non-cash-releasing • Ranking of benefits by key stakeholder • Outline of benefits realisation plan
6 Have the main risks been identified, alongside arrangements for their management and control?	• Business risks • Service risks • Likely probabilities and impact (high, medium or low) • Outline of risk management strategy
7 Have the key organisational constraints and business dependencies been identified?	• Evidence of critical path • Related programmes and projects • Assessment of internal and external constraints.

Key review criteria	Evidence required
Economic case	
8 Have the CSFs for options appraisal been identified?	• Prioritised CSFs (high, medium or low) • Relevant performance measures

9 Has a sufficiently wide range of options been identified and assessed within the long list?	• Use of any feasibility study
	• 10 to 12 main options
	  – full description
	• Use of the options framework
	  – options for business scope
	  – options for potential solutions
	  – options for service delivery
	  – options for implementation
	  – options for funding

10 Has a preferred way forward been identified following robust analysis of the available options?	• SWOT analysis of available options using:
	  – investment objectives
	  – CSFs
	  – benefits criteria
	• Evidence of likely support from key stakeholders and that it meets their objectives

11 Has the preferred way forward been unpacked within a short list for further examination and appraisal?	• Minimum of four options, including:
	  – do nothing or do minimum
	  – PSC

Commercial case	
12 Has a high-level assessment of the potential and its likely acceptability to the supply side been undertaken?	• Description of potential deal • Market soundings • Existing service providers
Financial case	
13 Has a high-level assessment of affordability and source(s) of required funding been undertaken?	• Indicative costings (£) • Likely sources or organisational funding
Project management case	
14 Has a high-level assessment of the achievability and deliverability of the project been undertaken?	• Indicative time-scales • Outline procurement strategy • Project management methodology
15 Are all the necessary arrangements in place for the successful completion of the next phase?	• Project board and reporting arrangements • Project manager and team • Project plan and agreed deliverables • Budget allocation and resources

Stage: Review of the OBC
Purpose: To establish VFM, procurement strategy and source of supply for the proposed solution.

	Key review criteria	*Evidence required*
1	Are the SOC investment objectives and planning assumptions still valid?	• Are they set at an appropriate level and SMART: − specific − measurable − achievable − relevant − timely • Still supported by stakeholders and customers
2	Do the services to be procured in the SOC still provide best fit in relation to organisational needs?	• Organisational context • Existing and future changes in needs • Expected changes in volumes and mix of services • Other existing, planned or possible services • Security and confidentiality issues
3	Have any outstanding differences at SOC stage between stakeholders and customers been satisfactorily resolved?	• Continued stakeholder commitment and involvement • Communication strategy
4	Has the assessment of likely benefits, risks, constraints and dependencies in the SOC been revisited and examined in further detail?	• Updated benefits criteria − benefits study • Updated risk assessment − risk study • Ongoing assessment − business strategies and plans

Economic case

5	Were the long-listed options in the SOC revisited and subjected to further scrutiny?	• New options • CSFs revisited • Options ranked, weighted and scored
6	Were the short-listed options in the SOC revisited and subjected to robust analysis?	• Economic appraisals for shortlisted options, including: − do nothing or do minimum − PSC − PFI (PPP) solution(s) • Use of appropriate tools: − sensitivity analysis − risk (£) quantification − evaluation of qualitative benefits (rank, weight and scoring) • Treatment of costs and benefits in accordance with Treasury 'Green Book' rules

Key review criteria	*Evidence required*

7 Has the PSC been constructed and assessed in accordance with HM Treasury guidance?	• Realistic solution capable of implementation
	• Risks identified, apportioned and measured for all project stages:
	  − design
	  − build
	  − finance
	  − operate
	• PFI (PPP) costs, where available

8 Does the preferred option represent best VFM or the most economically advantageous offer?	• Rigorous use of investment appraisal tools and techniques • All assumptions recorded • Achievable benefits streams • Stakeholders and customers support

Commercial case

9 Is there sufficient scope for a potential deal, which will meet organisational needs whilst offering best VFM?	• Potential for innovation within the provision of services and solutions • Potential for risk transfer in Design, Build, Finance, Operate stages • Potential for new business and alternative revenue streams • Likely contract length

10 Has the potential deal been considered in sufficient detail? The **how** rather than **what**.	• Preparation of OBS
	  − core, desirable and optional services
	  − delivery time-scales (phased improvements etc.)
	  − potential payment mechanisms
	  − ownership of residual assets
	  − service levels and performance measures

11 Is there a clear understanding of the business change agenda?	• Change management plans • Proposed mechanisms and milestones • Assessment of personnel implications
12 Is the potential deal still likely to be acceptable and bankable within the private sector?	• Market research and surveys • Use of HM Treasury standard contractual terms and conditions • Benchmarks − similar projects

Financial case

13 Is the solution still likely to be affordable?	• Financial appraisals for preferred option, including full assessment of:
	  − capital and current requirements
	  − net effective on prices
	  − impact on balance sheet (FRS5 etc.)
	  − income and expenditure account
	• stakeholder and customers agreement

Key review criteria	*Evidence required*

Project management case

14 Has the procurement strategy for the successful delivery of the required services been considered and prepared in sufficient detail?

- Consideration of procurement options, including:
  - use of EC directives
  - use of preferred bidder
  - OJEC notice
  - evaluation criteria and strategy
  - negotiations strategy
- ITT
- procurement plan and timetable
- draft OJEC

15 Are all the necessary arrangements in place for the successful completion of the next phase?

- Project methodology
  - PRINCE
  - project board and structure
  - project manager and team
  - project plan
  - project resources and budget
  - reporting mechanisms
- Use of external advisers
  - legal
  - financial
  - other
- Outline arrangements for:
  - benefits study and realisation plan
  - risk management strategy and plan
  - change management strategy and plan
  - contract management
- Arrangements for evaluation:
  - peer reviews
  - OGC gateway reviews (if required)
  - project implementation reviews
  - post-evaluation reviews
- Contingency plans

Stage: Review of the FBC
Purpose: To make the investment decision in respect of the most economically advantageous offer

	Key review criteria	Evidence required
1	Does the recommended deal still provide synergy and best fit with other parts of the organisation's business strategy?	• Notification of any changes during negotiations • Ongoing evaluation of business strategies and plans
	Strategic fit	
2	Does the recommended deal still satisfy OBC investment objectives and business needs?	• Notification of any changes during negotiations • Written confirmation of agreement on part of stakeholders and customers
	Investment objectives and business outcomes	• Change control arrangements
3	Does the recommended deal still provide all of the required services – both current and future?	• Notification of any changes during negotiations
	Related service requirements and outputs	– additional services – agreement of stakeholders and users – business justification and CBA

Economic case

4	Was a wide range of bids received from service providers in response to OJEC?	• Assessment of earlier assumptions • Use of evaluation criteria – long list of suppliers – short list of suppliers • Description of each bid received at BAFO • Method of treatment for varying bids • Basis for selection of preferred bidder (if applicable)
5	Was the most economically advantageous offer selected?	• Preparation and assessment of economic appraisals for: – do nothing/do minimum – revised PSC – best and final offers and/or – preferred bidder (if selected) • Use of appropriate tools: – sensitivity analysis – risk (£) quantification – evaluation of qualitative benefits (rank, weight and scoring) • Treatment of costs and benefits in accordance with Treasury 'Green Book' rules.

Key review criteria	Evidence required

Commercial case

6   Can the selected service provider deliver the required deliverables and services?

- Outline of the agreed deal
  - services − current and future
  - delivery time-scales
    - design
    - build
    - operate
  - payment mechanisms
    - performance and availability
    - volume and usage
    - incentives
    - future change
  - new business and alternative revenue streams
  - ownership of residual assets
  - service levels and performance measures
- Business, technical and cultural fit
  - track record

7   Have negotiations resulted in a robust and legally enforceable contract?

- Use of specialist adviser(s)
- Use of standard terms and conditions
- Key contractual terms agreed

8   How will business and service change be delivered and implemented successfully over the lifespan of the contract period?

- Assessment of known and expected change;
- Formula for handling unexpected change
  - benchmarking
  - market testing arrangements

Financial case

9   Is the proposed investment still affordable?

- Financial appraisals for recommended deal, including full assessment of:
  - capital and current requirements
  - net effect on prices
  - impact on balance sheet (FRS5 etc.)
  - income and expenditure account
- Stakeholder and customers agreement
- Confirmation of finance directorate

Project management case

10   Was the procurement undertaken in accordance with EC/GATT regulations and accepted best?

- Overview of procurement process
- Deviations from procurement strategy
- Use of legal and procurement advice (internal and external advisers)

11   Have the business and cultural implications of the intended service been fully understood and taken into account?

- Agreed programmes for:
  - change management
  - business process re-engineering
- Staff-side representation
- Personnel implications

	Key review criteria	*Evidence required*
12	Are all the arrangements in place for the successful implementation and delivery of the required services?	• Contract management strategy, including disputes resolution procedures • Skilled contract management team • Agreed schedules for service streams and outputs
13	How will the benefits be delivered and associated business and service risks managed throughout the lifespan of the service?	• Detailed benefits realisation plan • Robust risk management strategy • Monitoring and reporting arrangements – registers and regular audits

14	Are all the necessary arrangements in place for post-project evaluation?	• Agreed arrangements for evaluation:
		  – peer reviews
		  – OGC gateway reviews (if required)
		  – project implementation reviews
		  – post-evaluation reviews

15	Are contingency plans in place should the recommended deal fail at any stage?	• Contingency plans • Arrangements for regular review

Content of a SOC, OBC and FBC

Strategic Outline Case (main emphasis on strategic case and economic case)

Phase 1: Initial scoping

Primary purpose:

- To establish the case for change and strategic fit with other programmes and policies.
- To indicate the way forward in broad terms.

Structure and content

1 Executive summary

2 The strategic case

Strategic context

Organisational overview

- Snapshot of the organisation: purpose, structure and environment, etc.

Business strategy and objectives

- Existing and future business drivers, including any relevant national initiatives and stakeholders/customers for services

Other relevant organisational strategies, e.g. human resource

- Existing and future plans

Strategic needs

Investment objectives

- Key objectives for proposed investments

Existing arrangements

- Snapshot of current service arrangements (strengths and limitations)
- Business needs – current and future
- Service gaps to be filled

Outline Business Case (count all 5 cases in 'outline' terms)

Phase 2: Planning the investment

Prior to OJEC (pre-procurement)

Primary purpose:

- To validate the preferred way forward and identify a preferred option.
- To demonstrate value for money, affordability and achievability.

Structure and content

1 Executive summary

2 The strategic case

Strategic context

Organisational overview

- Update as required

Business organisational strategies

- Update as required

Other strategy and objectives

- Update as required

Strategic needs

Investment objectives

- Investment objectives ranked in order of priority and made SMART

Existing arrangements

- Update as required

Business needs – current and future

- Update as required

Desired scope and service requirements

- Detailed description of business outcomes and service outputs/requirements

---

Full Business Case (address all 5 cases in detail)

Phase 3: Selection of solution

Following competition (pre-contract)

Primary purpose:

- To select the service solution.
- To finalise post-procurement arrangements.

Structure and content

1 Executive summary

2 The strategic case

Strategic context

Organisational overview

- Update as required

Business organisational strategies

- Update as required

Other organisational strategies

- Update as required

Strategic needs

Investment objectives

- Update as required

Existing arrangements

- Update as required

Business needs – current and future

- Update as required

Scope and service requirements

- Update as required

Benefit criteria

- Update as required

Potential scope and service requirements
- Business scope and high-level service outputs

Benefits sought from investments (including benefit criteria)
- Main benefits by key stakeholder groups

Strategic risks
- Key business, service and external risks, together with outline risk mitigation and management strategy

Constraints and dependencies on investment objectives
- Internal and external

3 The economic case

Critical success factors (CSFs) and benefit criteria

Potential options
- Long-list for SWOT analysis, including 'do nothing' or 'do minimum' options
- Conclusion from SWOT analysis (including reasons for rejection of options)
- Short-listed options and results of high level assessment of costs, benefits and risks
- Recommendation of preferred way forward (including reason for recommendation)

Benefit criteria
- Main benefits by key stakeholder groups – ranked in order of importance and/or weight

Strategic risks
- Update as required, including specific proposals for mitigation and management

Constraints and dependencies
- Update as required

3 The economic case

Critical success factors (CSFs) and benefit criteria
- Update as required

Potential options
- Revisit and update, as required, including options not identified earlier

Preferred way forward
- Revisit and update, as required

Short-listed options
- Detailed description and review of short-listed options, including 'do nothing' or 'do minimum' and public sector comparator
- Results of economic appraisals for each option, including costs, benefits and risks retained under each short-listed option

Strategic risks
- Update as required

Constraints and dependencies
- Update as required

3 The economic case

Critical success factors (CSFs)
- Update as required

Main business options
- Summary of OBC options

Preferred way forward
- Summary of OBC conclusion and update as required

Short-listed options
- Detailed description of short-listed options, including 'do nothing' or do minimum', the PSC and service providers' solution

NPC/NPV findings
- Results of economic appraisals for each option, including costs, benefits and cost of risk retained

Also includes in very general terms

4 Commercial case
- High-level assessment of possible deal marketing capacity and other and supply-side issues

5 Financial case
- High-level assessment of affordability (including affordability and envelope)

Appraisal of non-financial benefits
- Results from weighting and scoring analysis for each short-listed option

Risk assessment
- High-level assessment of risks retained under each short-listed option, including indicative costing of design, build, finance and operational risks

Sensitivity analysis
- Results of sensitivity analysis undertaken for short-listed options

Preferred option
- Recommended option following above analyses

4 The commercial case
For possible deal (in outline):
Potential scope and services
Potential charging mechanisms
Potential key contractual arrangements
Potential personnel implications
Potential implementation time-scales
Potential accountancy treatment

5 The financial case
For possible deal (in outline):
Potential capital requirement
Potential net effect on prices
Potential impact on balance sheet
Potential impact on income and expenditure account
Overall affordability

Benefits appraisal
- Results of rank, weighting and scoring the qualitative benefits for each short-listed option, including service providers' solutions

Risk assessment
- Full assessment of risks retained under each short-listed option, including costing of DBFO risks

Sensitivity analysis
- Results of sensitivity analysis undertaken for short-listed options

Preferred option
- Recommended solution following above analyses

4 The commercial case
For recommended deal:
Agreed scope and services
Agreed charging mechanisms
Agreed key contractual arrangements
Agreed personnel implications
Agreed implementation time-scales
Agreed accountancy treatment

5 The financial case
For recommended deal:
Capital requirement
Net effective on prices
Impact on balance sheet
Impact on income and expenditure account
Overall affordability

6 Project management case
- High-level assessment of achievability and project management arrangements

7 Recommended way forward

Possible appendices
1 Analysis of long-listed and short-listed options (including reasons for rejection and selection)

6 Project management arrangements
Procurement strategy
- Intended method of procurement, including use of:
  – EC/GATT regulations
  – evaluation criteria
  – selection of preferred bidder
Project methodology and structure
Proposed project plan
Proposed use of advisers

Possible appendices
1 Economic appraisals
2 Financial appraisals
3 Sensitivity analysis

6 Project management arrangements
The procurement process
- Description of procurement process
- OJEC notice (attachment)
- Summary of ITN
- Prequalification: long- and short-listing of service providers
Communication strategy
Arrangements for contract management
Agreed benefits realisation plan
Agreed risk-management strategy
Arrangements for post-project evaluation
Contingency plans

Possible appendices
1 Economic appraisals
2 Financial appraisals
3 Sensitivity analysis

Key components of the NPV method

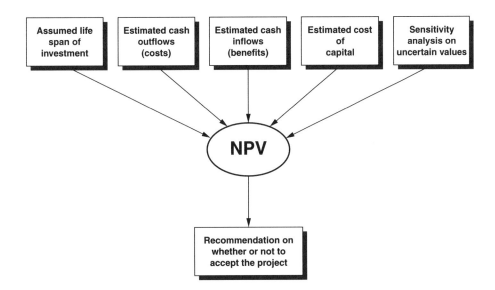

Glossary

Annuitising	Converting a sum of capital to an equivalent series of future annual payments or costs.
Commercial case	*See* 'five-case model'.
Discount rate	The annual percentage rate used to convert cash flows arising in future years to its present value.
Discounted cash flows	The stream of costs and benefits of an option discounted by the appropriate discount factor to show their present values.
Economic case	*See* 'five-case' model.
Equivalent annual cost	The constant annual costs which are equivalent (same present value) to a project's actual costs.
Financial case	*See* 'five-case model'.
Five-case model	A systematic framework for decision making. The framework ensures that the preferred option which results from the various analyses satisfies the following crucial tests: applicability to business needs and strategic direction (strategic case), optimises value for money (economic case), attractive to the marketplace (commercial case), affordable to the organisation (financial case), and achievable in terms of time-scale, resources and other business parameters (project management case).
Full Business Case	The document prepared in accordance with the 'five-case model' to validate and develop the preferred option identified prior to and during the tendering stage.
Internal rate of return	The discount rate which would give a project a net present value of zero.
Net present value	The difference between the present value of a stream of costs and benefits.
Nominal rate of return	A rate of return which includes a factor for the effects of inflation, and which should be applied to nominal (inflated) future cash flows.

Opportunity cost	The value foregone by not using a resource in the best alternative use.
Options framework	A systematic framework to facilitate comprehensive identification and assessment of options.
Outline Business Case	The document which builds on the strategic outline case and aims to identify a preferred option with indicative costs, benefits and risks.
Project management case	*See* 'five-case model'.
Public sector comparator	A 'reference project' showing the costs, benefits and risks of meeting the requirements in the output-based specification through a publicly funded solution. This solution should not mimic the private sector's solution(s).
Real price	The nominal or cash price deflated by a suitable price index.
Residual value	The expected market value or net asset value after depreciation of an asset (whichever is lower) at the end of its economic life.
Risk	The variability of outcomes from a decision, e.g. variability of returns from an investment decision. It is normally measured by statistical measures of standard deviation.
Sensitivity analysis	Analysis of the effects on an appraisal of varying the values of important variables to establish whether the preferred option is robust.
Strategic case	*See* 'five-case model'.
Strategic Outline Case	The document prepared to define the strategic context, objectives, scope and options for meeting the business need for an expenditure proposal.
Sunk costs	Costs that have already been incurred and irrevocably committed.

Further reading

Becker G (1976) *The Economic Approach in Human Behaviour*. University of Chicago Press, Chicago.

Central IT Unit (2000) *Successful IT: modernising government in action*. Cabinet Office, London.

Drummond MF *et al.* (1999) *Methods for the Economic Evaluation of Health Care Programmes*. Oxford University Press, Oxford.

HM Treasury (1997) *Economic Appraisal in Central Government: a technical guide for government departments*. HMSO, London.

National Audit Office (2001) *The Implementation of the National Probation Service Information Systems Strategy*. NAO, London.

National Audit Office (2000) *Report on the Millennium Dome*. The Stationery Office, London.

National Audit Office (1999) *Examining the Value for Money of Deals Under the Private Finance Initiative*. The Stationery Office, London.

National Health Service Executive (1999) *Public–Private Partnerships in the NHS: the private finance initiative*. NHS Executive, Leeds.

National Health Service Executive (1994) *Capital Investment Manual*. NHS Executive, Leeds.

NHS Executive (1995) *Information Management and Technology*. HSG 95(48). NHS Executive, Leeds.

Smith C (1999) *Making Sense of the Private Finance Initiative: developing public–private partnerships*. Radcliffe Medical Press, Oxford.

Smith C (2000) *Maximising Value for Money: examining the role of strategic outline cases*. Public Services Productivity Panel and Department of Health, London.

Treasury Taskforce (2000) *How to Construct Public Sector Comparators*. HM Treasury, London.

Treasury Taskforce (1999) *Standardisation of PFI Contracts*. HM Treasury, London.

Treasury Taskforce (1999) *How to Account for PFI Transactions*. HM Treasury, London.

Treasury Taskforce (1998) *How to Appoint and Manage Advisers*. HM Treasury, London.

Treasury Task Force (1998) *A Step-by-Step Guide to the PFI Procurement Process*. HM Treasury, London.

Treasury Taskforce (1991) *How to Appraise and Work with a Preferred Bidder*. HM Treasury, London.

Useful websites

- www.treasury-projects-taskforce.gov.uk
- www.open.gov.uk/
- www.detr.gov.uk
- www.ogc.gov.uk
- www.gcat.co.uk
- www.scat.co.uk
- www.citu.gov.uk/itprojectsreview.htm.
- www.doh.gov.uk/nhsexipu/strategy/index.htm
- www.nao.gov.uk

Index